Lucy

Other works by Damien Atkins

Good Mother

Lucy

DAMIEN ATKINS

PLAYWRIGHTS CANADA PRESS
TORONTO • CANADA

Playwrights Canada Press
The Canadian Drama Publisher
215 Spadina Ave., Suite 230, Toronto, Ontario, Canada M5T 2C7
phone 416.703.0013 fax 416.408.3402
orders@playwrightscanada.com • www.playwrightscanada.com

For professional or amateur production rights, please contact
Rena Zimmerman at Great North Artists Management Inc.,
350 Dupont St., Toronto, Ontario, Canada M5R 1V9 416.925.2051

The publisher acknowledges the support of the Canadian taxpayers through the Government of
Canada Book Publishing Industry Development Program, the Canada Council for the Arts, the
Ontario Arts Council, and the Ontario Media Development Corporation.

Front cover photo of Miranda Cocoran courtesy of
Scott Thornley, Sugino Studio, and the Canadian Stage Company.
Back cover photo of Seana McKenna as Vivian and Meg Roe as Lucy
in the Canadian Stage Company production by Chris Gallow.
Production Editor and Cover Design: Micheline Courtemanche

Library and Archives Canada Cataloguing in Publication

Atkins, Damien, 1975-
Lucy / Damien Atkins.

A play.
ISBN 978-0-88754-909-0

I. Title.

PS8551.T526L83 2010   C812'.6   C2010-902067-7

First edition: June 2010
Printed and bound in Canada by Canadian Printco, Scarborough

for Andrew

and

for Seana

ORIGINS

The only thing I knew when I started work on *Lucy* was that I wanted to write about autism. Through a remarkable series of coincidences, I had become acquainted with a teacher who worked with children with autism, and I was lucky enough to spend some time in his class. The children were astonishing. They were brilliant and frustrating—sometimes completely present and sometimes very distant. I decided to write about a little girl with autism, a little girl I started to call Lucy.

Almost immediately, I started to feel anxious. I did not want to condescend to this little girl. I wanted to get the details of her autism correct, but I didn't want her to be a victim, I wanted to avoid writing a play about *rescuing* her from her condition. Almost unconsciously I had stumbled into a growing debate in the autism community between those who want their autistic children to be normalized and those who want them to be valued for who they are, unchanged.

At the same time, I'd begun to imagine another character: a woman with a fractured, complicated relationship to the world. Vivian did not feel like she fit in anywhere, did not feel like she *belonged* anywhere. She was wrestling with a profound ambivalence about her fellow human beings. There was a great push and pull in her, I imagined, between wanting to connect with the world and wanting to shut it out entirely. Moreover, this ambivalence extended to her feelings about her own motherhood.

This was, frankly, alarming. The mothering instinct had always been a potent and unstoppable force in my writing—primal and undeniable. And here was a woman, a mother, who did not seem to have any instinct for it. I will admit that I was not sure where this was all coming from. But the more I wrote, the more I had to admit that I had a great deal of sympathy for Vivian, and at least some of her views on the world and the people in it. I suspected (hoped!) that I was not the only one to harbour such sharp, troubling doubts in my darker moments. Vivian scared me, mystified me, but I loved her.

So here were two women, related by blood—one young and one not so young—about whom I was feeling very protective. They were an odd pair. But something about it felt right. Vivian would be the mystery, Lucy would be the sleuth. The play would be told from Lucy's point of view, so that it would be difficult (for author and audience) to condescend to her in any way. She would, in her own way, take care of Vivian. She would be our narrator, our guide. And Lucy would not be a victim. She would, in fact, be a hero.

Lucy had its world premiere at the Canadian Stage Company's Berkeley Street Theatre on March 7, 2007 with the following company:

Vivian	Seana McKenna
Lucy	Meg Roe
Gavin	Tony Munch
Julia	Philippa Domville
Morris	Brendan Murray

Directed by Eda Holmes
Set Design by Teresa Przybylski
Lighting Design by Andrea Lundy
Original Music and Sound Design by Marc Desormeaux
Properties Design by Mary Spyrakis
Stage Management by Marinda de Beer
Assistant Stage Management by Krista Blackwood

The play subsequently opened, with the assistance of the Sloan Foundation, at the Ensemble Studio Theatre in New York City on October 28, 2007 with the following company:

Vivian	Lisa Emery
Lucy	Lucy DeVito
Gavin	Scott Sowers
Julia	Keira Naughton
Morris	Christopher Duva

Directed by William Carden
Produced by James Carter
Set Design by Ryan Elliot Kravetz
Lighting Design by Chris Dallos
Sound Design by David Margolin Lawson
Properties Design by Troy Campbell
Casting by Janet Foster
Stage Management by Jeffrey Davolt
Assistant Stage Management by Michal V. Mendelson
Sloan Foundation Program Director: Doron Weber
E.S.T./Sloan Foundation Project Directors: Carlos Armesto, Graeme Gillis

A radio version of *Lucy* was produced by L.A. Theatre Works in October 2008 under the direction of Michael Hackett. It is available at the L.A. Theatre Works website: www.latw.org

The playwright acknowledges the assistance of the 2005 Banff Playwrights' Colony, a partnership between the Canada Council for the Arts, the Banff Centre for the Arts, and Alberta Theatre Projects.

PLAYWRIGHT'S NOTES

Throughout the script, overlapping dialogue is indicated by the use of a slash (/). When the slash appears in one character's dialogue, it indicates that the next speaker should begin speaking at that point. There is a great deal of overlapping and compounded overlapping speech in the script, to the point where some conversations will become confused and muddy. This is deliberate, and should be allowed to play for maximum dissonance and discomfort.

Some of the characters, particularly Gavin, have lines of dialogue that include incomplete thoughts followed by an em-dash and a period. This is to indicate that the speaker interrupts his own thought and abandons it. I have chosen this punctuation to differentiate these moments from those that contain a simple em-dash or an ellipsis; the effect is that the lines take on a rhythm that is halting and full of self-doubt.

There can and should be a great difference in Lucy's voice when she speaks to us and when she speaks inside the scenes. Within the scenes it should also be clear that Lucy is trying to communicate, even if we cannot understand what she is saying, and even if it comes out as a yell or a bark or a scream. Outside the scenes she can communicate with us however she likes.

I have written in specific reactions and behaviours for Lucy, but feel free to explore supplemental and complimentary behaviours, reactions, or sounds that are not necessarily scripted, as per your research. Every person with autism has a unique presentation of their symptoms—embrace this freedom. I will add to this a note of caution: while it is necessary that we see Lucy being challenged and vitally distressed by the events of the play, she is not helpless, or pitiable. She is, essentially, a resourceful and resilient little girl.

All of the stage directions that appear in the text are my own invention.

The play is broken up into scenes for clarity in the rehearsal hall, but the action of the play (as Lucy presents it to us) should be swift, fluid, and continuous.

CHARACTERS

VIVIAN *(mid-forties)*
JULIA *(late thirties)*
GAVIN *(mid-forties)*
LUCY *(thirteen)*
MORRIS *(early thirties)*

SETTING

The play is mostly set in Vivian's home in the city with some brief excursions to far-off locales (real and surreal). The set should be impressionistic and suggestive, not literal—even the rug if you wish. Minimal props. Most of the setting and transitions (as well as Lucy's perspective) are suggested through lighting and sound.

Act One

The stage is dark. A moment of nothing.

We hear a young girl's voice. It seems to be coming from all around us. She whispers.

THE VOICE Hello, *Homo sapiens*. My name is Lucy. I want to show you something.

A light starts to come up on LUCY.

LUCY Sometimes things happen. And sometimes they make sense to me, and sometimes they don't. Sometimes I have to watch them over again in my head. This is mostly how I understand things—I play them back over and over until I can see how they make sense, like a story. *She* tells me stories sometimes, *good stories*, and she knows how to tell them so that all the parts fit, all at once. And I go down, into my little cave, and put them in there—because it's the safest place to keep all my things. And I can look at them whenever I want.

LUCY steps forward a little.

I like the stories she tells me. But this time, *the story is about her.*

In the darkness, a woman has quietly made her way onto the stage, carrying a notebook, a pencil, and a sack. A light comes up on her.

Look at her. *Look at her!*

The woman is still. Breathing, looking off into the distance. She comes to life as she is described.

She is not tall or short. She has long hair, like me. She has dirt on her face. She forgot to wash her hands. She's outside.

As LUCY describes the scene, it starts to take shape on the stage.

Oh! Oh! Oh! There are nine hills behind her. *Dry.* No water, no water anywhere. And the sun and the grass and the colours are all mixed up, see? Isn't this a good story?

The woman runs her hands through her hair.

That's a good part. When she runs her hands through her hair. I like that part. Her hair looks soft, so soft. And look! Look at her eyes! Blue blue eyes like ice. My eyes are blue like ice.

> *LUCY watches. The woman (VIVIAN) runs her hands through her hair again. She sighs.*
>
> *The sound of a soft wind running through dry grass.*
>
> *VIVIAN crouches and packs her bag. She stands again, breathes.*

Now, look. Look who's here.

> *GAVIN enters behind VIVIAN. VIVIAN does not turn.*

VIVIAN I wish we could stay a little longer. This is such beautiful light.

> *GAVIN does not answer. A moment.*

In Ethiopia, the light was like this. Like it came from all around you.

> *VIVIAN shakes her head.*

My brain is buzzing.

> *A short moment.*

GAVIN Umm… Vivian?

> *VIVIAN does not answer.*

Vivian.

> *She turns.*

VIVIAN Oh! Jesus!

GAVIN Shit, sorry if I scared / you.

VIVIAN I thought you were someone else, / I was talking to, to someone else—

GAVIN I know, sorry, that was, that was awkward, I should've— But you looked so peaceful, I didn't / want to—

VIVIAN Okay, okay, that's okay, / I'm fine.

GAVIN I didn't mean to surprise you, really. *(beat)* So. It's good to see you, Vivian. Hi.

VIVIAN Hi.

GAVIN Hi. So, this is one of your anthropological digs, or, whatever?

VIVIAN   Uh, yes. Yes.

GAVIN   Can I?

> *GAVIN hugs her. She is stiff for a moment, then relaxes.*

VIVIAN   You're good at that.

GAVIN   I've heard.

VIVIAN   You have lines around your eyes.

GAVIN   So do you.

VIVIAN   I know.

GAVIN   You look beautiful.

VIVIAN   Oh. Thank you.

> *Beat.*

So.

GAVIN   I was surprised when I called your office and they said you were out west.

VIVIAN   Oh.

GAVIN   If I had known, I would have driven out earlier.

VIVIAN   Oh! That's… kind.

> *Tiny beat.*

Well…

GAVIN   I thought you might be done for the day.

VIVIAN   I don't think so, actually, I have some—

GAVIN   You're not going to make this easy for me, are you.

VIVIAN   What.

GAVIN   You haven't changed.

VIVIAN   Was I supposed to?

GAVIN   No, no, Viv, that's not what I mean. I mean I'm glad to see you, I'm, I'm comforted that you seem the same, and, everything that comes with that.

VIVIAN   Oh. Oh.

Beat.

GAVIN   Listen Vivian, can I take you out to dinner?

VIVIAN   What?

GAVIN   Come on, just like old times?

VIVIAN   Where?

GAVIN   I don't know, there must be somewhere, isn't there some little great place you like to go to?

VIVIAN   There's not much around here.

GAVIN   It is a little remote, isn't it. No one for miles.

VIVIAN   That's why I like it. Gavin—

GAVIN   So what do you think?

VIVIAN   You know what, I'm not sure this is a good time for a visit, or a, whatever—

GAVIN   Listen, I just want to talk to you!

VIVIAN   Well, you should've called.

GAVIN   I, well, I *did call,* I called several times, but I didn't want to leave a message, because, well, you never call me back anyway—

VIVIAN   I would have called back if it was an emergency.

GAVIN   You know, some things that aren't necessarily emergencies are still things that need, you know, a response—

VIVIAN   Gavin, please, you're… This is quite a shock, and I'm exhausted from a long day.

GAVIN   I tried very hard, actually, not to disturb your / work day.

VIVIAN   I'm busy. You should have left / a detailed message and I could have—

GAVIN   I didn't want to say what I have to say over the phone, I needed to see you in person. It's a long drive you know, so I, so that's why I hope you'll hear / me out—

VIVIAN   *Will you just get to the point?*

GAVIN   *I want to talk to you about Lucy.*

        Tiny beat.

VIVIAN   Well, okay. Well, we're going to have to do that another time because there's no way that I have the energy for that right now.

She starts fussing with her things.

GAVIN   Vivian, come on.

VIVIAN   What if I don't want to talk about her?

GAVIN   You read all my letters, Viv, I know you're interested—

VIVIAN   How do you know I read your letters?

GAVIN   Don't you?

VIVIAN   Well I'm not heartless, you know, / I'm not some sort of—

GAVIN   I never said that, Vivian, you know I never said that, *just listen to me.*

She stops.

Beat.

VIVIAN   I'm listening!

GAVIN   I'm gathering my thoughts!

Beat.

VIVIAN   Is she… all right?

GAVIN   Well, you know, it's been a couple of years since you've seen her, and—

VIVIAN   Yes, how is she, is she… progressing?

GAVIN   Well, some days I think so. It's just… She's thirteen. She's… well, she's thirteen, you know?

VIVIAN   No.

GAVIN   It's, you know… puberty. She's going through puberty, she's—. Listen, Vivian, I need you.

VIVIAN   You need me.

GAVIN   Yes, I was hoping you'd—. Look, it's just, like I said, Lucy's having a bit of a rough time—

VIVIAN   What?

GAVIN   —and, meanwhile, there's been a development in my life—

VIVIAN   Wait a minute—

GAVIN   Right, and I just need to, to talk to you about how Lucy fits into that development, you know?

VIVIAN   What are you—what do you mean?

GAVIN   Sorry, that's not the right—

VIVIAN   A development?

GAVIN   A person.

VIVIAN   *Oh.*

GAVIN   That's what I wanted to talk to you about.

>   *Beat.*

VIVIAN   *(quietly)* I am so stupid.

GAVIN   What?

VIVIAN   Congratulations.

GAVIN   Thanks, I— It's taken me a long time to find a, a—

VIVIAN   Person.

GAVIN   Yes, so. We're getting married.

VIVIAN   Oh.

>   *Beat.*

GAVIN   Viv, listen. I need a break. I need a, well, I need a serious break. Lucy is brilliant, you know, she's fantastic, and I love her, but it's just been me all this time, at least until, until Sarah came along, and really, when she came along it was like a, a, a miracle you know, to suddenly be, be not alone, or whatever, and I just, I need some time to be with that, to have a life, and spend some time with Sarah, and just, and just figure out what my life is, you know what I mean?

VIVIAN   You need me, what does that mean: you need me.

GAVIN   Oh, come on, Viv, you know what I'm getting at. Now that Sarah's in the picture, it seems like a good time to—

VIVIAN   Why don't you just say what you want, *stop dancing around it, just say what it is you came here for.*

GAVIN   I want you to take Lucy.

>   *Beat.*

VIVIAN   What?

GAVIN   *(quickly)* There's a school out east, in the city, and it would really, really benefit Lucy, it's a real good place, really respected. So I applied for her, and she's been on the waiting list for three years, but this year she got accepted, and we have to take it or we go back to the bottom of the—

VIVIAN   How long?

GAVIN   A year?

VIVIAN   A *year*? No.

GAVIN   She needs to be there at least a year to have any real chance of— And, and after a little bit I can come up, for a week or two here and there, or whatever, or Christmas—

VIVIAN   No. / No. A *year*?

GAVIN   Don't do that, Vivian, don't just say no without actually thinking about it. I know it's a big deal, / but you have to at least think about it—

VIVIAN   She has problems, Gavin, there's things that I don't know how to do, I'm not equipped to deal with, with all the, / the doctors and the tests and her therapy and—

GAVIN   Look, look, I *know* you can do this. And you'll have the school, and the doctors will help you figure out all the—

VIVIAN   We had an agreement.

GAVIN   But, but, things *change*, you know, and, and, I've tried not to ask for much, you know Vivian, and I've appreciated the financial, you know, help. It's just, you haven't seen her in a while, Viv, you don't know what's been going on, I think she could really use some—

VIVIAN   We had an *agreement*, Gavin.

GAVIN   Yes, but you visited, *that* wasn't part of the agreement, I didn't *make* you do that, you *wanted* to, and I thought—

VIVIAN   That's not the point, *that's not the point,* / and you know it!

GAVIN   Listen, listen, listen, she's slipping away from me, Vivian, she doesn't really talk to me anymore, and she gets scary sometimes, it's like she's going *backwards*, and I'm afraid I'm screwing this up because I don't know what parts of it are just puberty and normal and what parts of it aren't, and she needs better therapy than I can get for her out here, or it'll screw up her development, and she'll be fucked up for the rest of her life, and, and I *know* you can do this, and, and I'm *exhausted*, Vivian, *I'm fucking exhausted.*

VIVIAN   *(quietly)* I can't.

> *GAVIN starts to cry.*

> *Beat.*

Please don't do that.

> *He cries.*

Please.

> *Beat.*

Gavin.

GAVIN   I know you're scared, Vivian. But, but she needs you. She needs her mother. *That's gotta mean something to you.*

> *Beat.*

VIVIAN   *(quietly)* It does.

> *Beat.*

GAVIN   Vivian, I know you can handle this. Please. I need this. Lucy needs this.

> *She looks at him.*

VIVIAN   You would trust me?

> *Lighting shift.*

SCENE TWO

> *LUCY in a spotlight. The sounds of the city flood the stage. Loud. Honking horns, voices, sirens.*

LUCY   *(out)* Gavin says I can hear things like a dog. But I'm better than a dog, much better! Can a dog hear people whispering across the street? I can hear my brain humming! Sometimes it's too much, too much! I can hear my toenails growing! I can hear a spider crawling across the ceiling! I can hear through walls!

The lights come slowly up on VIVIAN's *house in the city. It is large and clean and impersonal. Bare walls.* VIVIAN *is staring off.*

JULIA *(cheerful and rapid)* I think that's everything. I laid out the rest of it on your desk. If you have any questions, just ask. Oh, and I found that cross-reference you were looking for. It's not the Broome, it's the Dawkins. Proud of that one, took me hours. I pulled it, and highlighted the relevant sections. It's on your desk.

> *Beat.*

Vivian.

> VIVIAN *does not answer.*

(lightly) Vivian… You've gone away again!

VIVIAN Sorry. What?

JULIA You've gone away again!

VIVIAN I'm right here.

JULIA I know.

> VIVIAN *shakes her head.*

VIVIAN Sorry.

JULIA Oh! Here. I need you to see this. *(She displays a few sheets of paper.)* For some reason the computer invented its own date and time stamps, so all of these are marked January 1904, but Randy says that's an easy fix. And I'm sure we can get more resolution from these photos. We're missing some of the details.

VIVIAN Good eye.

JULIA And I pushed back our meetings to next week, as you requested.

VIVIAN Thank you, thank you. You, you don't miss a thing.

> JULIA *laughs, embarrassed.*

JULIA So. I'm so glad you're back! Are you glad to be back?

> *Tiny beat.*

VIVIAN Um.

JULIA No?

VIVIAN Sure.

JULIA   You miss it.

VIVIAN   Yes.

JULIA   I don't know how you do it. I just, I only spent a few weeks out there and I thought I'd *expire*. I mean, I know there isn't any traffic out there, or smog, or screaming and sirens, but didn't it just wear you down? The lack of, of modern conveniences?

VIVIAN   Like what.

JULIA   I don't know, corner stores.

VIVIAN   Oh. No.

>   *Beat.*

JULIA   Sorry.

>   *VIVIAN shakes her head.*

It's an adjustment.

VIVIAN   Yes.

>   *Tiny beat.*

JULIA   *(laughing)* Listen, home isn't so bad, Vivian. The city! Living people! Clean toilet seats!

VIVIAN   I guess.

JULIA   Good. Listen, while I'm here, there's some grant stuff we should go over—

>   *The doorbell rings.*

VIVIAN   What time is it?

JULIA   Do you want me to get that?

VIVIAN   Oh, you have to go. I'm sorry, you have to go.

JULIA   Oh, okay, I didn't mean to—

VIVIAN   No, no it's not your fault, it's just, *they're early*—

>   *The doorbell rings again, repeatedly.*

GAVIN   *(from off)* Lucy, don't.

VIVIAN   Coming! Are you ready to go?

JULIA   In a sec, I just have to—

VIVIAN   I'll help you.

JULIA   My God, Vivian, don't worry about it. Listen, why don't I just—

> *JULIA opens the door. GAVIN is standing there with a couple of*
> *big suitcases.*

GAVIN   *(looking off)* Lucy!

JULIA   Hello.

> *He turns to her.*

GAVIN   Oh! I'm Gavin.

JULIA   Hi. Julia.

> *Small beat.*

Can I / help you?

GAVIN   Um, is Vivian…?

JULIA   Sure, she's—

> *VIVIAN finishes tidying.*

VIVIAN   Here, I'm right here. I didn't, you caught me off guard.
We agreed seven.

GAVIN   Did we? I don't think so.

VIVIAN   Yes we did, I was going to be more ready. Seven.

GAVIN   If you say so, I guess I made good time on the, the… Um, sorry
about the doorbell. Lucy has a thing…

JULIA   Lucy?

GAVIN   Um, our daughter, yeah.

VIVIAN   Where is she?

GAVIN   She ran back to the car. I let go of her hand for a second and—
(looking back) She's nervous. *(to JULIA)* Sorry, I forget your name?

JULIA   Julia.

GAVIN   Oh right. Gavin. *(indicating the bags)* Umm, I guess I should…

> *He starts bringing the suitcases in.*

VIVIAN   Are these all hers?

GAVIN   No, one of them is mine.

VIVIAN   How long are you staying?

GAVIN   Well, I have to see her through the transition. I don't know, till Saturday, Sunday?

VIVIAN   I thought you said a couple of nights.

GAVIN   I guess I meant five or six. Okay, six. I'll sleep on the floor in Lucy's room, don't worry.

VIVIAN   I wasn't—. I'm worried about her in the car.

GAVIN   Car's a safe place.

VIVIAN   Gavin.

GAVIN   Relax, Viv, I cracked the window.

VIVIAN   What's that supposed to mean?

GAVIN   It means she's okay as long as she can hear me. *(yelling off)* Lucy, can you hear me?

LUCY   *(from off)* No!

GAVIN   Uh oh, she's mad. Jesus, that's a long drive. Four days!

VIVIAN   You could've flown, I would've—

GAVIN   I know, I know, I didn't want to risk it. So this is your house!

VIVIAN   Yes.

GAVIN   Don't you have any stuff?

VIVIAN   Stuff?

GAVIN   I don't know, art.

VIVIAN   I'm never here. Gavin…?

GAVIN   All right, I'll go get her. I'll be a minute. She likes the car.

    He goes. An uncomfortable moment.

JULIA   So!

    Beat.

    So Lucy's your…

VIVIAN   I know he told me seven.

JULIA   I'm sure it's okay.

> *VIVIAN nods.*

This will be nice for you!

VIVIAN   Yes.

JULIA   How long do you get to have her?

GAVIN   *(from off)* Ow! Lucy, co-operate! ow!

VIVIAN   Oh, a while. A year.

JULIA   Oh, that's so great.

VIVIAN   Yes.

JULIA   I had no idea. I'm sorry, I never thought to ask—

VIVIAN   No, no, that's okay.

JULIA   Well, I'm, I'm anxious to meet her.

VIVIAN   Listen, Julia—

> *She is interrupted by GAVIN, who appears again at the doorway. LUCY has been following along right behind him.*

GAVIN   Here we are. She's so nervous. Hey Lucy. She loves this shirt. Lucy, enough, I want you to say hello.

> *He steps aside. LUCY is standing there, suddenly exposed. An attempt has been made to dress her up. It has been less than successful. She is wearing sunglasses.*

Take off the sunglasses, that's not polite.

> *LUCY makes no movement to do this. GAVIN pulls them off her face. She starts blinking and flinching.*

Lucy, say hello. Go on.

> *They wait.*

Now, Lucy.

> *They wait.*

> *LUCY studies VIVIAN in her periphery.*

Philippa Domville as Julia, Meg Roe as Lucy and
Seana McKenna as Vivian in the Canadian Stage Company production.
photo by Chris Gallow

VIVIAN   Hello, Lucy. Remember me?

> *A moment.*

> *LUCY scampers away and runs around the room.*

LUCY   Listen! Lucy! House! *(She makes a face.)*

GAVIN   Lucy! She's used to more colour, I guess. And mess. Still, that's... Lucy that's terrible.

LUCY   Lucy, that's terrible.

GAVIN   You should apologize.

> *LUCY runs over to the rug and lies on it, staring down.*

Okay, good enough I guess. *(to JULIA)* Foreign territory, you know.

JULIA   Is she all right?

> *LUCY is pressed up against the rug.*

GAVIN   She's going to love that rug. *(to JULIA)* Um, she's fine, she's autistic.

JULIA   Oh, good. I mean, sorry, I didn't…

GAVIN   Oh, Vivian didn't—

JULIA   Yes of course, I remember, sorry. *(beat)* Lucy is a beautiful name.

GAVIN   Yeah, Vivian thought we should name her after the, uh…

JULIA   The Hadar find.

GAVIN   Oh hey, you're a fossil freak too.

JULIA   Sort of.

GAVIN   Wow, great.

> VIVIAN *has been staring at* LUCY.

VIVIAN   She's not upset?

GAVIN   Uhhh, I don't think so.

VIVIAN   Does she need anything?

GAVIN   Why don't you ask her.

> VIVIAN *nods. She starts to creep over to* LUCY. GAVIN *looks at* JULIA.

Big house.

JULIA   It is, isn't it.

VIVIAN   Lucy?

JULIA   *(to GAVIN)* Do you want something to drink or something?

GAVIN   No thanks, I'm good. Sorry, you're Vivian's…?

JULIA   I'm her, I'm her assistant. Research.

GAVIN   Oh.

VIVIAN   Lucy?

GAVIN   New book?

JULIA   Yes. Absolutely.

GAVIN   Been quite a few years since the last one, hasn't it.

JULIA   Has it?

GAVIN   Um.

JULIA   We're working on it. Vivian's the best.

GAVIN Yeah.

> *VIVIAN is down on the floor near LUCY.*

VIVIAN Lucy?

> *She reaches out a hand to touch her, lightly. LUCY shrieks, a blood-curdling howl. VIVIAN recoils. JULIA jumps. GAVIN does not react.*

What did I do? What did I do?

GAVIN If you're going to touch her, it's better if you're firm.

VIVIAN What?

GAVIN If you're too gentle it freaks her out. That's a bit of a rule.

JULIA *(quietly)* Jesus.

VIVIAN *(shaken)* I forgot! I forgot, you could've—

GAVIN Yeah, I've made you a list, you'll get used to it.

> *VIVIAN nods.*

Hey listen, why don't you show me to Lucy's room?

VIVIAN Oh. All right.

JULIA I guess I should be—

VIVIAN Yes, thank you.

GAVIN Actually, Julia, can you…?

JULIA Oh! Well…

GAVIN Thanks.

> *GAVIN and VIVIAN exit with the bags.*
>
> *Beat.*
>
> *LUCY looks up. She stands. She looks around.*

JULIA Hello.

> *LUCY doesn't answer.*

They're just upstairs. My name is Julia.

> *No response.*

It's nice to meet you. You're very pretty.

LUCY closes her eyes and starts to moan softly. It is a strange, sad, animal sound.

Vivian?

JULIA hesitates a moment and then comes over to her. She puts a hand on her shoulder. LUCY flinches.

Oh right.

JULIA kneels down and hugs LUCY to her, very tightly. She rocks her side to side. LUCY's moans subside a bit.

Mommy and Daddy will be right back. They'll be right back. Shhh.

They rock. Finally LUCY is silent.

VIVIAN enters, stares.

JULIA notices her and stands.

She was crying.

Lighting shift.

SCENE THREE

The middle of that night. LUCY in a spotlight.

LUCY   *(out)* Gavin says her name is Vivian. He says she came for dinner and he had to remind me to be nice. He opened the door and I was spinning and she was there. She had boots on! And we had mashed potatoes for dinner, and she gave me a puzzle because I was only six. Then she left, and Gavin sat in the big chair and there was water on his cheeks and he said time for bed, time for bed. Her name is Vivian, he says. Remember? You know her.

Lights up on VIVIAN's house. LUCY is drawing busily. GAVIN is with her, holding her pencil crayons. VIVIAN has just entered.

GAVIN   Did we wake you? *(looks at his watch)* Aw jeez, it's after midnight, sorry.

VIVIAN   I wasn't... I haven't been sleeping.

GAVIN   Oh.

VIVIAN   I don't want to interrupt.

She makes to leave.

GAVIN   No, no, it's good. Stay.

She does.

Beat.

VIVIAN   Is this a ritual?

GAVIN   No, I'm just letting her adjust. She'd probably prefer I wasn't here, but—

VIVIAN   Uh huh.

GAVIN   She's only happy when she's working. Remind you of someone?

VIVIAN   I'm not the only one.

GAVIN   She didn't get the genius gene from me.

VIVIAN takes the box of pencil crayons.

VIVIAN   These look well-used.

GAVIN   You'll have to replace them about once a week. You have to get this brand, so memorize the box.

VIVIAN   Okay.

GAVIN   She never uses the white one.

VIVIAN   The white one?

GAVIN   Never figured that one out.

VIVIAN sits down. They both watch LUCY for a moment.

So! You've been busy.

VIVIAN shrugs.

Work treating you okay?

VIVIAN   I suppose.

GAVIN   You suppose.

VIVIAN   Well, it's a one-sided relationship at present.

GAVIN   What does that mean.

VIVIAN   It means I haven't found anything.

GAVIN   What are you talking about, you wrote a book!

VIVIAN   That was synthesis. Analysis of other people's finds, a few *minor* fossils on my part.

GAVIN   Ah.

VIVIAN   So.

> *Beat.*

Does Lucy get along with your...

GAVIN   With Sarah?

VIVIAN   Yes, Sarah.

GAVIN   Yeah, Sarah's great with her.

VIVIAN   Good.

GAVIN   Yeah, she loves kids, she'd like a few more.

> *Beat.*

VIVIAN   What... what does she do.

GAVIN   She's a travel agent. We're going to take a cruise.

VIVIAN   Oh! You always wanted to travel.

GAVIN   Oh, you think you know me. I'm afraid of boats.

VIVIAN   Oh. *Right.*

> *VIVIAN shakes her head. GAVIN smiles.*

GAVIN   Don't get me wrong, she's great, she's great, we're a, we're a good fit. You know... we go to movies, she cries, she wants to be held, I like that. She gets jealous of other women, I have to prove to her that she's the one I want. I like all that. We're a good, uh... fit.

> *Tiny beat.*

VIVIAN   Is she... jealous of me?

GAVIN   Why should she be jealous of you? That was fifteen years ago.

VIVIAN   Oh.

> *GAVIN laughs.*

What's so funny?

GAVIN   Of course she's jealous of you. You gave me a child, she hates you.

VIVIAN   Oh. She can take a number.

GAVIN   What does that mean?

>   *VIVIAN shrugs.*

Come on, Vivian.

VIVIAN   What do you mean *come on.*

GAVIN   I mean we've only had a handful of quick visits since—. And you know how you are—

VIVIAN   What do you want?

GAVIN   I want to know *how you've been.*

>   *A moment.*

VIVIAN   Why don't you give me that list.

>   *GAVIN smiles.*

GAVIN   Okay.

>   *He pulls out a tattered folder and hands it to her.*

The main thing is routine. She likes routine, she needs it. You have to set one up and stick to it. If you don't stick to it, she'll act out. That means she can get violent with you or with herself. Wakes up at six thirty. So *you* wake up at six thirty. Oatmeal for breakfast, always the same kind, and five slices of banana and some brown sugar. Sorry, *(He makes a note on the page she is staring at.)* that should be two tablespoons of brown sugar. Then, washes her face, brushes her teeth, brushes her hair, in that order. Twenty minutes of playtime before school. She likes to spin, but watch her in the mornings or she'll throw up her breakfast. *(He is turning pages.)* We had a routine at school: I took her to the doorway and said goodbye there. I stayed in the doorway until she said hello to the teacher and then she looked back, and she expected me to be there. She might want to try this routine with you. Whatever you set up, stick with it. End of the day, pick her up in the same spot. Take the same route home every day—she'll be reading the signs. TV after school—cartoons if you can find them, if not that, then anything other than the news. Right, dinner. *(He flips some pages for her.)* Nothing too hot or too cold, nothing that crunches. You'll have to be clever with vegetables. Uh, she does her homework after dinner, oh and you need to supervise this or she'll draw instead.

VIVIAN All right.

GAVIN *(flipping a page)* There's more. After homework she takes a bath, she hates that, she'll do anything to get out of doing that, but a bath is easier than a shower, which is impossible. Make sure the water is tepid, and make sure she has her light blue towel.

VIVIAN You packed that?

GAVIN Yes, I packed it. I think. After the bath she reads a book—right now her favourite is *Suspension Bridges of the World,* it's in her suitcase. She'll read it forever if you don't take it away and hide it. And after she reads she goes to bed.

VIVIAN You do this every day.

GAVIN There's a whole other section on weekends.

> *VIVIAN is silent.*

(continuing) You're stuck with that rug now, you're gonna want to have it cleaned pretty regularly. She likes low sounds like whispers, and that sort of thing. She doesn't like sharp sounds, with one exception.

VIVIAN The doorbell.

GAVIN Yes. *(He smiles.)* The thing is, Vivian, you might not get a lot of return. She might not pay much attention to you. You have to understand that. You have to know that she might not seem very affectionate, or grateful. Okay?

VIVIAN Okay.

GAVIN It's only for a while. You're going to do fine.

> *VIVIAN nods.*

Can you watch her? I need to sleep.

VIVIAN Okay.

GAVIN Don't let her escape.

VIVIAN Escape?

GAVIN That was a joke.

> *VIVIAN looks at him.*

She's not a monster, Viv.

VIVIAN I know.

GAVIN   Okay, okay. Good night.

VIVIAN   Good night.

> *GAVIN starts to go.*

GAVIN   Thanks for doing this.

> *VIVIAN nods.*
>
> *GAVIN lingers in the doorway.*
>
> *A tiny moment.*

I've missed you, Vivian.

> *VIVIAN is silent.*

I don't know, I'm tired.

VIVIAN   Go to sleep.

> *GAVIN nods and exits. LUCY continues to draw. VIVIAN pulls out the white pencil crayon and looks at it a moment.*

Why bother. It doesn't make a mark.

> *LUCY looks at VIVIAN.*
>
> *Lighting shift.*

SCENE FOUR

> *A spotlight. LUCY steps into it.*

LUCY   *(out)* Do you want to know what is excellent?

> *LUCY spins.*

Try this! Try this! But, but, keep your eyes open and you will get to see all the colours all at once and around they go and everything mixes until you can't recognize anything anymore, everything moves so quickly, you could be anywhere, anywhere anywhere, anywhere! You should really do this if things are different and you don't recognize them. Everything looks the same this way! Try this try this try this try this!

> *The lights come up to reveal the house. It is a little over a week after the previous scene. LUCY is spinning. She has a backpack on. VIVIAN comes in the door.*

VIVIAN   You know, it's polite, when someone asks you a question—

> *LUCY stops spinning and throws herself down on the carpet.*
>
> *Beat.*

Well, so. How was your day. How was school?

> *No answer.*

Lucy?

> *VIVIAN crouches over LUCY.*

Lucy, how was your day at school?

> *No answer.*

Are you hungry?

> *LUCY gestures.*

Is that a yes or a no?

> *LUCY gestures.*

Okay. How was your day at school.

> *A moment. Hesitantly,* VIVIAN *lays down opposite* LUCY *in the same position.*

Can you hear me? Lucy?

> *She gets up.*

Okay sit up now. Time to sit up. Time to answer questions.

> *LUCY gestures.*

If you don't sit up you don't get TV.

> *LUCY sits up.*

Oh, *selective* hearing. Interesting.

LUCY   Interesting.

VIVIAN   How was the school? Are you liking the school?

> *LUCY won't look at her.* VIVIAN *tries to get her attention but* LUCY *flinches.*

Fine, we don't have to look at each other, just— *(She speaks to LUCY without looking at her.)* How was— This is ridiculous. How was school.

LUCY   Ummm... *(giggles)*

VIVIAN   Do you like your teachers?

>   *LUCY giggles.*

Did you learn anything today?

>   *LUCY gives a short bark.*

No, don't do that.

>   *LUCY giggles.*

It's an expensive school, they better teach you something—

LUCY   *(suddenly)* A whale is a mammal, not a fish! Why didn't you finish your ants on a log, she thinks she doesn't have to listen to us, now is not the time for talking please, hands folded, look at me please, you did very well today Lucy. Don't! Don't! Please hold down the lever when flushing!

VIVIAN   That's—. That's very good, Lucy.

LUCY   You name Lucy!

VIVIAN   What? No. My name is Vivian.

LUCY   My name is Vivian.

VIVIAN   No, I mean—

LUCY   You name Vivian.

VIVIAN   Yes.

>   *VIVIAN puts a hand out to touch her but LUCY recoils.*
>
>   *VIVIAN gets up, starts to take her things into the other room.*

Are you hungry yet?

>   *She exits. LUCY turns on the TV and takes off her pants. VIVIAN returns.*

Lucy, what are your pants doing on the floor.

>   *No answer.*

Look at me.

>   *She does not. VIVIAN goes around to the other side of her.*

Lucy, put your pants back on.

>   *LUCY goes to the TV. She turns the sound up.*

Don't do that. Please put your pants on.

VIVIAN turns the TV off.

People wear pants. Clean people wear pants.

VIVIAN goes to her. LUCY evades and turns on the TV.

Don't do that!

VIVIAN turns the TV off.

Let's be serious. I'm taking care of you, I'm responsible for——. You have to wear pants. *(LUCY skitters away. VIVIAN follows.)* You're my responsibility, you have to do what I say! *You have to do what I say!*

LUCY cowers, hands over her ears.

I'm not going to hurt you. I wasn't——. But you have to listen to me, you can't just——. Let's put your pants on.

LUCY grimaces. VIVIAN pulls up LUCY's pants.

Good.

LUCY pulls her pants down.

Okay, you know what? That's it for the TV. No TV tonight. Now put your pants on, or you'll lose something else, too.

LUCY   Silence please!

VIVIAN stops.

VIVIAN   Pardon?

LUCY   Silence please!

VIVIAN   Don't be silly, that's——. Here.

She goes to grab LUCY. LUCY gasps and skitters away.

LUCY   Silence please!

VIVIAN   Don't make me chase you.

LUCY   Silence please! Silence please!

VIVIAN   That's very rude. Come here.

LUCY   SILENCE PLEASE!

VIVIAN moves toward LUCY. LUCY giggles and wriggles away.

VIVIAN   This is not a fun game!

LUCY   Silence please!

>   *VIVIAN chases LUCY until she has her cornered.*

Lucy gets to watch TV.

VIVIAN   No, not when you misbehave.

LUCY   Silence please!

VIVIAN   Come here. *(VIVIAN corners her.)* Come on now. Let's put your pants on.

>   *There is nowhere for LUCY to go. VIVIAN starts to put her pants back on her. LUCY submits, moaning.*

LUCY   Lucy gets to watch TV.

VIVIAN   Well, you can't.

LUCY   Silence Lucy please!

VIVIAN   No, you're going to the bathroom and you're going to go wash your hands. Then we're going to have a nice, calm dinner.

>   *LUCY makes a face.*

I can make faces, too. Go.

>   *LUCY exits to the bathroom. VIVIAN clears up LUCY's things. A beat. There is some thumping from the bathroom.*

Lucy? What's going on in there? Are you washing your hands?

>   *No answer.*

Lucy? Lucy, come out here!

>   *LUCY emerges. Her hands are dirty.*

What's that on your…? *Lucy?* What did you…?

>   *She is gone. Beat.*

(off) Lucy!

>   *VIVIAN runs back on.*

Lucy, did you do that?

>   *LUCY covers her ears.*

Why would you do something like that?

LUCY starts to moan.

Listen to me, *who's supposed to*—

LUCY moans louder.

That's very very… That's *horrible*, who's going to clean that up?

LUCY starts to yell. She starts to bang at her head.

Lucy! Don't! DON'T DO THAT!

LUCY gives herself one great whack. The stage goes black.

SCENE FIVE

A voice from the darkness.

MORRIS   Hello, Lucy. Nice to meet you. You can call me Morris. Do you want to draw? Here you go, here's some paper, and some crayons. *(beat)* There, she seems calmer already.

The lights start to come up again. We are in MORRIS's office. It is a short time later. LUCY is drawing. VIVIAN is standing, agitated.

VIVIAN   I'm sorry to disrupt your / evening.

MORRIS   Please don't apologize.

VIVIAN   No, no, I'm not, this is not my—. Anyway, I know that our appointment is tomorrow, but it was, it seemed like it was an emergency, there was really no option.

MORRIS   It's no trouble. I was looking forward to meeting you tomorrow and to get a chance to get started today was just, just okay. / I'm glad you thought to call, to rely on us. You can, that's why we—

VIVIAN   I mean it was bad enough, she was misbehaving, and I wasn't sure what sort of, uh, strategies to be employing, to get her to— You know, it's confusing! She'll be laughing and then suddenly she's screaming, or, or, she's *hitting* herself! She was *hitting* herself, *hard*, and I couldn't figure out why she was doing it, or how to get her to stop—

MORRIS   Right.

VIVIAN   —and I certainly wouldn't want anyone to think that I—

MORRIS   *(with a tiny smile)* Vivian. No one thinks that.

VIVIAN   Good.

>   *Beat.*

>   Good. Thank you.

MORRIS   *(kindly)* That must have been quite a shock for you.

VIVIAN   Oh! The…

MORRIS   Yes.

VIVIAN   Yes.

MORRIS   And the…

VIVIAN   Oh, yes.

MORRIS   You were alarmed.

VIVIAN   Alarmed, *yes.*

>   *They are nodding at each other.*

MORRIS   It's strange, isn't it, your beautiful little girl, and suddenly she does something so primitive.

VIVIAN   Yes.

MORRIS   Uh huh. Can you remember if you said anything upsetting to her?

VIVIAN   What? No. Other than "go wash your hands"? No.

MORRIS   What was your posture.

VIVIAN   I don't know, crouched.

MORRIS   Crouched. Were you trying to hold on to her?

VIVIAN   No, I was trying to put her pants on.

MORRIS   Oh, she lets you touch her?

VIVIAN   Not really.

MORRIS   Yeah, she doesn't really seem like a hugsy kid.

VIVIAN   Hugsy?

MORRIS   Can touch but doesn't like to be touched. Sounds like she's—

VIVIAN   Tactile defensive.

MORRIS   Yes. That would also account for the running away. *(He smiles at her.)* You've been doing some reading.

VIVIAN   A little, I—

MORRIS   `You're an expert!

VIVIAN   I never said that I was an expert.

> *He starts rifling through a thick file.*

MORRIS   I'm only teasing. The theoretical side is easier to manage than the reality.

VIVIAN   Yes.

MORRIS   That's why I'm here. Listen, on her routine list here it says she watches TV after school. Did she get to do that?

VIVIAN   You have her routine list?

MORRIS   Yes, your husband sent it with Lucy's file.

> *He holds the file up.*

VIVIAN   Oh.

MORRIS   Did she get to watch TV?

VIVIAN   No.

MORRIS   Why not?

VIVIAN   She was misbehaving.

MORRIS   Right off the bat?

VIVIAN   Well, she took off her pants, and she wouldn't put them back on again, and I thought I should—

MORRIS   Are those new pants?

VIVIAN   Why. Yes.

MORRIS   I'm guessing she hates corduroy. *(to LUCY)* I don't like corduroy either. *(to VIVIAN)* It's called sensory integration dysfunction. This would cause her to under-react to some stimuli and overreact to others. Corduroy is probably very painful for her.

VIVIAN   Corduroy wasn't on the list.

MORRIS   We'll add it then.

VIVIAN   If she didn't like it, why didn't she say something?

MORRIS   She did! But you misunderstood her communication. So you said no TV.

VIVIAN   Right.

MORRIS   This was an interruption in her routine, she got upset, you weren't getting it, so she went to the bathroom and made it plain.

VIVIAN   Made it—? She smeared her feces all over the walls!

MORRIS   The general intent was plain even if the specifics of the complaint were not. Listen, kids have two basic areas of control: what goes in and what comes out. She used what she had to let you know she was upset.

VIVIAN   You can't be serious.

MORRIS   Don't you have routines that you like to follow?

VIVIAN   Yes, but—

MORRIS   Do you get upset when they're interrupted?

VIVIAN   They're being interrupted right now!

MORRIS   And?

He is smiling at her. She is silent.

Is there anything else you can tell me about the episode?

VIVIAN   Well, it seemed like a game to her, she was giggling.

MORRIS   Uh huh, emotions are confusing for autistic kids. She might be having an emotion and not sure what the appropriate expression is for that emotion.

VIVIAN   Oh.

MORRIS   I want to try something. *(He brings out a chart with some faces on it.)* Lucy? Lucy.

VIVIAN   She hasn't been speaking much.

MORRIS   Uh huh. Lucy?

LUCY   Silence please.

MORRIS   Lucy, look at me, please.

She looks at him out of her periphery. He uses his hands to indicate that she should look him in the eyes.

Christopher Duva as Morris and Lucy DeVito as Lucy
in the Ensemble Studio Theatre production.
photo by Carol Rosegg

Look at me, please. How do you feel today?

LUCY   Lucy, don't!

> *She turns away.*

MORRIS   Nope, look at me, please.

> *He turns her face to his.*

How do you feel today? Do you feel happy? *(He points to the happy face.)*

LUCY   Silence please.

VIVIAN   That's rude.

LUCY   That's rude.

MORRIS   Do you feel sad?

LUCY   You feel sad.

MORRIS   No no. This is sad. *(He points to the sad face.)* Do you feel this way?

LUCY looks away.

Look at me. Do you feel frustrated?

LUCY   You feel frustrated.

MORRIS   How do *you* feel? Frustrated? *(He points to the frustrated face.)*

LUCY   How do *you* feel?

MORRIS   Lucy, look at me. Can you tell me how you feel?

LUCY   That's rude.

MORRIS   Can you show me which one of these faces you are?

LUCY yells. He waits. She stops.

Are you done?

She yells again.

I don't like yelling.

She yells again, stops.

He waits. She yells. He waits. She is silent.

Okay, thank you.

He starts writing in the file. VIVIAN waits.

So! Written any new books lately?

VIVIAN   Pardon?

MORRIS   I enjoyed the first one, very much. You're quite something.

VIVIAN   Oh, thank you.

MORRIS   I suppose you read about the Dikika baby.

VIVIAN   Yes, of course.

MORRIS   It's quite a find! Afarensis, isn't it?

VIVIAN   You're an expert!

He looks up. He laughs.

MORRIS   Yes, well. This is, this is a real pleasure. I can't wait for your next book.

VIVIAN   Me too.

MORRIS   Uh huh. Well, listen, if she tantrums again, look at her immediate circumstances: what stimulus is bothering her? Taste, touch, sight, smell, sound. Something that is vaguely noticeable to you and me but awful for her. Do what you can to get her not to hit herself. If that's impossible, we'll get her a helmet.

VIVIAN   A helmet.

MORRIS   Yep. And I'm going to ask you not to let her spin. Spinning lets her tune out.

VIVIAN   Okay.

MORRIS   I'm also going to give you this to take home with you. *(He hands her the face recognition chart.)*

VIVIAN   Oh, I, why?

MORRIS   It's just something she needs to get going on, needs to practise. She's a little behind, so—

VIVIAN   How do I know what the faces are?

MORRIS   Well, it's pretty—. It's labelled on the back.

VIVIAN checks one of the faces.

VIVIAN   That's "frustrated"?

MORRIS   Yep.

VIVIAN   It looks like "suspicious."

MORRIS   Oh, well—

VIVIAN   And this is going to help her get better, get more… communicative?

MORRIS   Absolutely, definitely. She needs to be able to tell us how she feels. And if we can get her to do that, then we can work on getting her to understand how *other people* are feeling.

VIVIAN   Right.

MORRIS   It's called theory of mind. It's what allows you and I to understand that other people may be thinking or *feeling* something that we are not. People with autism can have trouble putting themselves in your shoes, that's why they can seem incapable of compassion, they can seem—

VIVIAN   Cold.

MORRIS   Yes. Good.

MORRIS starts leafing through the file.

VIVIAN   My ex-husband sent in that file?

MORRIS   Yes.

VIVIAN   What's in it.

MORRIS   Lots of things, technical things. It looks like Lucy hasn't had a lot of access to any enlightened therapies. This is odd, I have all of your ex-husband's information, but there's not a lot in here about you.

VIVIAN   He used, he used to handle all the particulars.

MORRIS   Great! Well, listen, since you're here, I have a questionnaire that we need to go through, just some regular questions we ask of any of our new parents.

VIVIAN   What kind of questions?

MORRIS   Just the basics, doctor information, medical history, family history—heart disease, depression, you know…

VIVIAN   Oh.

MORRIS   It'll just take a few minutes. Half of Lucy's genes are yours, we should check them out a little.

VIVIAN   Uh huh.

MORRIS   I'm sure they're brilliant!

VIVIAN   Why don't I take that home and fill it out.

MORRIS   Are you sure? It's nothing major, we can just—

VIVIAN   I'd really prefer to take it home. *(to LUCY)* Lucy, I think it's time to go.

MORRIS   Oh, okay, sure.

VIVIAN   I'll fill it out when I have some time.

MORRIS   Great. Oh yes, and let me give you this booklet so we can get started on some mimicking exercises.

VIVIAN   Mimicking. Who is she supposed to mimic?

MORRIS   Well, me. And you, most of the time.

VIVIAN   Uh huh. *(to LUCY)* Lucy, let's go. *(to MORRIS)* That works, does it? That seems…

> *LUCY stands up and pulls down her pants.*

MORRIS   In my opinion, it helps, yes.

VIVIAN   Lucy! Lucy, I know you don't like the pants, we'll change them when we get home, but you have to wear them now.

> *LUCY does not respond.*

Okay…

> *VIVIAN goes to her.*

MORRIS   I know it sounds odd, but mimicking is really one of the best ways for her to learn.

> *VIVIAN is trying to pull LUCY's pants up. LUCY resists.*

VIVIAN   Lucy…

MORRIS   You're her mother, she identifies with you, she looks up to you—

LUCY   Silence please!

MORRIS   So she's going to want to start behaving like you—

> *VIVIAN is still struggling.*

VIVIAN   Really.

MORRIS   You're the best shot she has of learning to function normally.

LUCY   That's rude!

VIVIAN   Please, Lucy—

MORRIS   Do you need some help?

VIVIAN   Yes!

> *MORRIS intervenes, manages to help VIVIAN get LUCY's pants up.*
> *LUCY yells at them.*

I don't like yelling!

> *LUCY screams and lies on the floor.*

Jesus Christ.

> *Beat.*

MORRIS   Are you okay, Vivian?

VIVIAN   *I'm not the patient here.*

MORRIS   Of course not.

Beat.

Listen, I'm sorry if I overwhelmed you. It's natural to feel overwhelmed, you're the primary caregiver. And we have a lot of challenges, and a lot we want to accomplish with your daughter. But you've come to the right place. We're on the cutting edge here, we have the best resources, we have the smartest people.

VIVIAN nods.

Lucy's been allowed to retreat into her disability. All I want is for her to join us out here in the real world. All right?

Beat.

VIVIAN   All right.

MORRIS   Good. Vivian. Trust me.

Lighting shift.

SCENE SIX

VIVIAN's home. LUCY in a spotlight.

LUCY   *(out)* I think I'm dying. I'm swelling up like a balloon. Like there are rocks in my stomach, churning and rubbing together, pressing out. My head hurts. I never knew what the bath was for until now. It's the only thing that helps. To press back on the rocks, to plug up my ears so my brain doesn't leak out. I want to lie in the bath for a hundred hours until I soak up all the water, until I look like a pink fruit, until my eyelids shut and my mouth closes over and I float to the bottom and there is no aching no aching just humming humming humming.

We hear the distorted sound of a doorbell one room away. Then two voices. The lights come up slowly as the sound crystallizes. JULIA has just come in the door.

JULIA   Is this a bad time?

VIVIAN   Um.

JULIA   Because you can say if it is, but if it isn't, I brought some stuff that I need to go over with you. And I didn't want you to feel like I was ambushing you with work, *(She produces a couple of wine glasses.)* so I'm going to do my best to make sure you don't notice.

VIVIAN   Oh.

JULIA   Okay?

>   *JULIA jiggles the glasses.*

VIVIAN   Okay.

>   *JULIA starts opening the wine and gestures to some folders.*

JULIA   Here, you look at these while I do this. There's a couple of different digs for us to choose from, so I put together a short list.

VIVIAN   Right.

JULIA   And we had another couple of calls from the publishers—

VIVIAN   They're just going to have to wait.

JULIA   —so I talked them in circles until they were exhausted.

VIVIAN   Thank you.

JULIA   No need. *(short beat)* I think Randy's getting depressed, not having you around the lab as much. It's been strange.

>   *VIVIAN looks up at her.*

VIVIAN   Are you checking up on me?

JULIA   What, no.

VIVIAN   What are people saying? Are people saying something?

JULIA   No, it's just unusual for you, in particular, to—

VIVIAN   What are they saying? Did they send you?

JULIA   Vivian, no, I'm—. Look, I, honestly, I'm here as a friend. I just thought you might like some company.

VIVIAN   Oh.

JULIA   Come on, have you never surprised a friend in need with a cheap bottle of wine before?

VIVIAN   No.

JULIA   Oh. *(She laughs.)* Well, first time for everything. All right?

VIVIAN   All right.

JULIA hands her a glass of wine.

JULIA   Where's Lucy?

VIVIAN   In the bath.

JULIA   I thought she hated baths.

VIVIAN   She wanted one!

JULIA   How is she? Does she like her new school? Do you like her new doctor?

VIVIAN   I suppose.

> *Beat.*

JULIA   *(a kind laugh)* Please. Elaborate.

VIVIAN   Well. Her therapy is pretty rigorous.

JULIA   Oh yeah?

VIVIAN   Charts, and punishments—sorry, *consequences*—smell jars.

JULIA   Really.

VIVIAN   To teach her to crave more… appropriate smells. It's… very involved.

JULIA   More involved than the other times?

VIVIAN   What?

JULIA   The other visits.

VIVIAN   Oh. I don't know.

JULIA   That school has a good reputation. If anyone can help Lucy, I'm sure they can.

VIVIAN   Yes.

> *Beat.*

What did you mean, a friend in need.

JULIA   What?

VIVIAN   That's what you said, a friend in need.

JULIA   Did I?

VIVIAN   Yes.

JULIA   I just meant… I don't know, am I wrong?

VIVIAN hesitates.

VIVIAN   No.

JULIA   Do you want to talk about it?

VIVIAN is silent. A tiny moment.

I'm going to make a confession.

VIVIAN   Oh.

JULIA   I hated you.

VIVIAN   What?

JULIA laughs.

JULIA   Not in any real sense, no, I just mean… Because your book came out just when I was finishing my thesis, and, and spending every night at the grad pub drinking beer with these Danish cultural anthropologist buddies of mine, anyway, just stupid—. It was, you know, typical, it was fine. I was fine, I was smart. I thought I had time. But you! But you, when your book came out, and it was all you, no co-authors, just you and Africa… And there you were, and you were barely older than me, and you were this, this huge—. And I realized you have one shot to be brilliant, and if you miss it… Anyway. It was important for me to—. But, but, the thing is, when I look at you, when I watch you work, I just know: this is where I was meant to be. Because *you're it, Vivian.* You're the standard. You're the visionary.

VIVIAN   You're embarrassing me.

JULIA   I'm not finished. *(indicating the wine)* More?

VIVIAN shakes her head. JULIA pours her some more.

And I just think, and I don't mean this to sound in any way presumptuous or condescending, because, anyway, I just think you shouldn't, you shouldn't doubt yourself so much. You'll find something. You'll find something! You'll make your discovery, you'll finish this book, and it will be genius. Whatever it is, it will be genius. I know it.

Beat.

VIVIAN   *(tentative)* I've been thinking of going back. Back to Africa.

JULIA   Africa.

VIVIAN   That's where the real work is.

JULIA   Okay, well. You know, Africa would be great, it's just going to take some real revising of our funding goals.

VIVIAN   I know, I know.

JULIA   But if that's what you want to do, that's what we'll do. We'll make it happen.

> *JULIA smiles.*

VIVIAN   Your enthusiasm is really… really admirable.

JULIA   You're not convinced.

VIVIAN   No, I—

JULIA   I'm sorry.

VIVIAN   No, it's not you.

JULIA   Oh, then—

VIVIAN   It's not the book, it's…

JULIA   …what.

VIVIAN   Never mind.

JULIA   Tell me.

> *Beat. VIVIAN looks at her warily.*

(*warm*) Go ahead. Please.

VIVIAN   It's me, I'm…

JULIA   What.

VIVIAN   It's getting worse.

JULIA   It's getting worse.

VIVIAN   *I'm* getting worse.

JULIA   Okay…

VIVIAN   I mean, I mean, I spend all of my time away, in the field, digging and sifting, and looking at fossils of mandibles and pelvises—

JULIA   (*encouraging*) Yes.

VIVIAN   —and molars and premolars, and theorizing about mortality rates and brain sizes and the kinds of lives these people must have led, and really, so much of it can seem so primitive and brutal, and I think "How did they survive?"

JULIA   Sure!

VIVIAN   And yet... when I come back to this, this... giant ashtray of a city, all I want to do is go back. Away from civilization. Go back and sift, and dig.

JULIA   And be alone.

VIVIAN   Well— Why do you say that?

JULIA   I don't know, just a sense. A look I see you giving people every once in a while.

VIVIAN   A look?

JULIA   Like they're in the way.

VIVIAN   Really.

JULIA   It's just an observation.

VIVIAN   Oh. Well. Okay, well, look, take my neighbour out here—she's clipped out a few press things about me and she, whenever she catches me outside she says "How are you?" as if she's been *wondering* how I am, as if she's just been *dying* to find out *how I am*, and she involves me in a twenty-minute conversation about what I'm currently doing, as if she really understands, or cares, or is capable of having an intelligent dialogue about it—

JULIA   Maybe she *is* interested—

VIVIAN   And all I want her to do is leave me alone, just leave me alone, because it feels like she's trying to, to open my stomach up and poke at my guts, or *something*—

JULIA   Huh.

VIVIAN   —and when she's done, when she's finished poking around, she waits for me to ask about her, *but I don't care, so I don't ask.* And I think maybe *now* she'll leave me alone. But of course she won't. The next time she catches me outside, she comes over again, with this "How are you?"—

JULIA   Isn't that just being polite?

VIVIAN   *Exactly*, she can't help herself! We're so jammed up against
each other here in the city, the landscape here is just other people,
there's nothing real, there's no nature, just more and more people, and
this noise, *this constant noise*. And people go crazy, but nobody thinks
"Why don't I just go away? Why don't I just go away where there is no
one else around to screw up my life because they don't have one?" *(beat)*
Is that shocking?

JULIA   N-No.

VIVIAN   Is it odd?

JULIA   Um.

VIVIAN   Anti-social?

JULIA   Well, it's in the neighbourhood.

> *Tiny beat.*

VIVIAN   Have you ever felt that way?

JULIA   I guess. I've never heard someone articulate it that way, but I guess
I've had... moments when I've felt that way, yes.

VIVIAN   *Moments.*

JULIA   Yes.

> *Beat.*

VIVIAN   I can't believe I told you that.

JULIA   It's fine.

VIVIAN   Listen, Julia. I don't have many friends. It's hard.

JULIA   *(kindly)* Most people find it hard to make friends.

VIVIAN   No, it's hard *having* friends.

> *JULIA puts her hand on VIVIAN. VIVIAN recoils.*

JULIA   Don't get the wrong idea, Vivian, I wasn't—

VIVIAN   No, I know, I know—

JULIA   I just, I just want you to feel safe, I want you to feel like you can—

VIVIAN   But *I don't*, I *don't* feel safe, Julia, I don't feel... *at home* anymore, in
my life, or maybe I never did, maybe I never did feel... *whatever*, but,
but *something* is happening to me, I feel like I'm cracking, or, or, or...

(She clenches her teeth and growls in frustration.) Every day, I... Every day I feel more and more—

> *There is a shattering scream from off. LUCY runs on in a towel.*

Lucy?

> *LUCY wails.*

JULIA   *Jesus.*

> *LUCY is running around, desperate.*

VIVIAN   Lucy, tell me what's wrong.

JULIA   Honey are you / okay?

VIVIAN   Lucy, you have to communicate.

JULIA   Can I do anything?

VIVIAN   This is just a tantrum. Use your words, Lucy, use your words.

JULIA   Vivian...

VIVIAN   That's what the doctors told me to do! *(to LUCY)* How can I help you until you tell me what's wrong?

JULIA   Vivian, she's having her period.

VIVIAN   What?

JULIA   I see some blood.

VIVIAN   *(freezing)* Oh. Oh God.

JULIA   Lucy. Lucy, come here.

> *JULIA intercepts LUCY. LUCY struggles, but JULIA is firm.*

Ohhh, okay. Okay. It's just your period, honey.

VIVIAN   *I didn't know.*

JULIA   Is this your first time, honey? Has this ever happened to you before?

LUCY   Lucy's dying!

JULIA   No you're not. *(to VIVIAN)* Do you have anything?

VIVIAN   Any what?

JULIA   A pad, *something*, do you have anything?

VIVIAN   I must have some.

Keira Naughton as Julia and Lucy DeVito as Lucy
in the Ensemble Studio Theatre production.

photo by Carol Rosegg

VIVIAN runs off.

LUCY   Lucy's dying!

JULIA   No you're not. Didn't anyone explain this to you?

LUCY   Blood on the floor!

VIVIAN runs back on.

VIVIAN   There's blood on the floor!

JULIA   Did you get it?

VIVIAN   Oh, uh—

JULIA   Vivian.

VIVIAN   I'm sure I have some under the sink.

JULIA   Okay, why don't you—

LUCY   Lucy's dying!

VIVIAN   Can you take her?

JULIA   Oh. All right, okay, Lucy, let's go to the bathroom.

JULIA takes her purse and takes LUCY off to the bathroom. LUCY cries. VIVIAN covers her ears.

VIVIAN   Please. Make it stop. Make it stop, *make it stop.*

JULIA   *(from off)* Can I use one of these towels?

VIVIAN   Yes!

LUCY wails.

I can't do this. I can't do this. *I can't do this I can't do this—*

LUCY wails again. VIVIAN covers her ears. The sound morphs into something deeper, something ominous and huge. It starts to rattle the house. The lighting shifts. VIVIAN looks around in terror as the sound mounts.

(wailing, trying to drown out the sound) I CAN'T DO THIS!

Abruptly the sound is gone and the lights are back to normal. JULIA has re-entered.

JULIA   Vivian.

VIVIAN doesn't answer.

Vivian!

VIVIAN   *(recovering herself)* Is she all right?

JULIA   Just scared. I think she wanted to be alone to get dressed. What happened?

VIVIAN   I'm—. *(She looks around and shakes her head.)* All that blood.

    Beat.

JULIA   Are you all right?

VIVIAN   *I don't know how to do this.*

JULIA   Don't overreact. This is just a bad day. You're just a little rusty.

VIVIAN   You don't know that.

JULIA   Yes I do. You're her mother.

VIVIAN   I'm not made for this, Julia, *I'm really not.*

JULIA   Don't be silly, Vivian.

VIVIAN   *(quiet) I never wanted a baby.*

    Beat. JULIA *is silent.*

And when I got pregnant I kept hoping for it to kick in, the *want* to have her, but it never did.

JULIA   That's just—

VIVIAN   And all the time she was growing inside me I just wanted her *out.* I didn't want to have to care for her. Everyone around me was congratulating me, and I was trying, I was *trying*, but it didn't feel right, I wasn't feeling what I was supposed to be feeling…

JULIA   Okay…

VIVIAN   And when she was born and they put her on my chest, *I knew*, I *knew* that it was wrong. I didn't know what to do with her. My body was running on automatic, it disgusted me.

JULIA   A lot of mothers go through that, Vivian.

VIVIAN   I watched my breasts produce milk, I watched myself hold her, and my brain was screaming "This is wrong! This is wrong! You don't know how to do this, you weren't meant to have children!"

JULIA   Vivian…

VIVIAN   So I left.

> *Beat.*

JULIA   *(quietly)* What?

VIVIAN   Just for a weekend. Which I *knew* I wasn't supposed to do, but I needed to clear my head, and I knew I had to figure it out alone because no one else would understand. And when I came back, Lucy didn't want my milk anymore, and Gavin never wanted to put her down. So I went away. To Africa. And Gavin pleaded with me to come back, and I thought I *would* come back, at some point, I thought I would… but the weeks passed… and it got harder and harder, and I just couldn't… and then months passed, and then… *years.*

JULIA   *Oh.*

> *Beat.*

(carefully) Vivian. Look. From what I know, autistic babies can be very frustrating, they don't give back any love, they don't giggle and laugh—

VIVIAN   No, it wasn't her. It was *me.*

JULIA   It was probably just postpartum—

VIVIAN   *No.* I have no instinct for this. I look at other women, Julia, and I… They seem to have a natural… Women who, women like you, who seem to, who seem to have a natural… *What's wrong with me?*

> *A moment.*

JULIA   Vivian, I—. Listen, I hear you, and I… I'm just trying to… It's—. I don't know.

> *Beat.*

VIVIAN   I understand.

JULIA   No, listen—

VIVIAN   I shouldn't have told you that. I shouldn't have made you listen to that.

JULIA   Vivian, I want to help.

VIVIAN   No, really, it's okay. You should go.

JULIA   I don't have to go.

VIVIAN   Yes, you should. You should go. I need to be alone. I think I need to be alone right now.

JULIA   Okay. Okay, if that's what you want.

> *JULIA heads for the door then turns back.*

Vivian, you… You're going to be fine. You're her mother.

> *VIVIAN looks away.*
>
> *JULIA exits.*
>
> *A moment.*
>
> *LUCY steps into the room. VIVIAN turns to her.*

VIVIAN   Lucy?

> *LUCY is staring at her curiously.*

How long have you been standing there?

> *Abrupt lighting shift.*

SCENE SEVEN

The middle of the night. VIVIAN's bedroom. Darkness. LUCY in a spotlight.

LUCY   *(excited, out)* Oh! Oh! Oh! My brain is exploding! So many things happening all at once and they don't get sorted until night, when everything is quiet. You-can-call-me-Morris says I am changing. I am going to be like her, he says. Ever since then, and ever since my blood, I want to look at her. So I go into her room at night quiet quiet like a quiet cat, and I look at her. This is the best time to do it, when she is still and all the parts fit. Something is changing! I am watching her face to see if she can feel it. I stare at her as hard as I can, through her eyelids, through her eyes into her deep deep brain, and it is dark in there and there are shapes like smoke you want to grab them! And then… *and then…*

> *From the darkness we hear a scratching. LUCY gasps and scampers out of her spotlight.*
>
> *A moment of silence.*

(whispering) Vivian! Vivian!

VIVIAN switches on a side light.

VIVIAN   Lucy?

LUCY   Are you awake?

VIVIAN   What are you doing in here?

LUCY   Are you awake?

VIVIAN   What's going on.

LUCY   I'm scared!

VIVIAN   Of what?

LUCY   *You know.*

VIVIAN   No, Lucy, what?

LUCY   Not what. *Who.*

> *There is a scratching noise somewhere. Maybe at the door.*
> *LUCY yelps, cowers.*

Did you hear that?

VIVIAN   No.

LUCY   Listen.

VIVIAN   This can't be—. This is— Why are you talking like that?

LUCY   Like what?

VIVIAN   I can't possibly be awake.

LUCY   You can't hear that?

VIVIAN   Lucy, maybe… maybe you should go.

LUCY   Just let me stay, just for a few minutes, please. I'm scared.

VIVIAN   There's nothing to be scared of.

> *LUCY jumps into the bed.*

LUCY   Tell me a story.

VIVIAN   What?

LUCY   Tell me a story.

VIVIAN   I don't know any good stories.

LUCY   What about my blood?

VIVIAN   You want a story about your... blood? About menstruation?

LUCY   Yes.

VIVIAN   I—. It's, it's really nothing to be afraid of... Every woman does that, every woman has that. Do you understand?

> *LUCY nods.*

More?

LUCY   Tell it like a story.

VIVIAN   I don't know how to—. Okay. Well, no one's really actually sure why we menstruate, why we evolved that way. Some people think that it has to do with keeping the womb clean and ready for fertilization. Other people think it's the body's way of fighting off infections that attach themselves to, to sperm. This isn't a good story.

LUCY   Yes, *go on.*

VIVIAN   And other people, they think that *whatever* it was for, it doesn't matter, because we may be evolving past it. Do you understand that? Everything evolves, everything moves forward. And if that's true then maybe women in the future won't go through it. Are you following?

LUCY   Yes.

VIVIAN   But for now we do, and, and it's something that we, that women, all have in common. Because we are responsible, as the female of the species, for incubating the offspring, the child, inside the womb. It's all very delicate, it's very complicated. But the womb is where the offspring, the fetus, the baby, gestates—grows, okay? And it has to be ready, it has to be clean. It has to be clean to make babies.

LUCY   Thank you.

VIVIAN   You're... you're welcome.

> *Beat.*

LUCY   I want to be alone. Just you and me. In a little cave.

VIVIAN   Why, Lucy.

LUCY   Because. They will never leave us alone.

VIVIAN   Who.

LUCY   People are terrible.

> *Scratching.* LUCY *freezes.*

Did you hear that?

VIVIAN   No.

LUCY   Maybe they won't notice us. Maybe they'll walk by.

VIVIAN   Who?

LUCY   Shhh.

> *Scratching.* VIVIAN's *head snaps toward the sound.*

Did you hear that?

VIVIAN   What the hell is—

MORRIS'S VOICE   Lucy? Vivian?

> VIVIAN *reacts.*

LUCY   You can hear it. You can hear it, too!

> *Scratching. It is starting to come from all around them, below and above them. A horrifying, penetrating sound.*

MORRIS'S VOICE   How do you feel today, Lucy?

VIVIAN   Who's there?

MORRIS'S VOICE   Do you feel happy?

LUCY   You see?

VIVIAN   Who's there? What's going on?

MORRIS'S VOICE   That's why they can seem incapable of compassion, they can seem—

VIVIAN   *Oh God.*

> *There is a low rumble, like the earth quaking beneath the house. The light flickers.*

LUCY   Make it go away!

JULIA'S VOICE   I don't understand you. How am I supposed to help you if you don't use words?

VIVIAN   What do you mean? I am! I am!

The rumble is getting louder. The walls rattle.

Stop it! Stop doing that!

MORRIS'S VOICE   Speak English, please.

VIVIAN   *I am speaking English!*

Louder rumble. VIVIAN *and* LUCY *cower.*

MORRIS'S VOICE   You're overreacting, Vivian.

VIVIAN   Go away!

GAVIN'S VOICE   Vivian, do you love me?

VIVIAN   Please! Go away!

LUCY   They will never leave us alone.

MORRIS, JULIA, *and* GAVIN'S *voices are starting to distort.*

MORRIS'S VOICE   How do you / feel today?

JULIA'S VOICE   How do you / feel today?

GAVIN'S VOICE   How do you feel today?

LUCY *screams.*

VIVIAN   Stop it! Stop it!

MORRIS'S VOICE   You're overreacting because your nerves are overstimulated.

VIVIAN   Go away!

The voices are distorting more and more.

MORRIS'S VOICE   What is wrong with me?

JULIA'S VOICE   And when she was born and they put her on my chest,
I knew—

GAVIN'S VOICE   She's not safe here, she's not safe here!

Their voices dissolve into a cacophony. The house shakes. The door rattles.

LUCY   HELP! HELP!

There is a blinding flash of light. The door flies open and light pours through it. We hear a hideous roar. A hundred languages at once. The house shudders.

VIVIAN   GO AWAY! GO AWAY AND LEAVE US ALONE!

She races over to the door and slams it shut. The roar disappears and the lights revert back to normal. VIVIAN *stands at the door, swallowing air.* LUCY *stares at her from the bed.*

LUCY   Vivian!

VIVIAN does not answer.

Vivian.

VIVIAN   *(dazed)* This is just a nightmare.

LUCY   Shhhh.

LUCY goes to her.

VIVIAN   *(quiet, to herself)* No, this isn't my life. This is just a nightmare. *I don't belong here.*

LUCY   Yes, you do.

VIVIAN   No, Lucy. This is just a nightmare. This isn't my life.

LUCY   *Yes.* Everything evolves. Everything moves forward.

VIVIAN looks at her.

VIVIAN   What?

Beat.

LUCY looks up.

LUCY   Oh! Look!

VIVIAN does. It is snowing.

What's that?

VIVIAN   *(stupefied)* It's *snow.*

LUCY   *(awed)* Oh. *White.*

VIVIAN   *This doesn't make sense.*

LUCY   It will. Don't be scared. Don't be scared, Mom. It will. You'll see. *It will.*

LUCY and VIVIAN watch the snow fall as the lights fade.

End of Act One.

Act Two

SCENE ONE

The stage is dark. A spotlight comes up on LUCY.

LUCY *(out)* I drew you a picture! This is me up here. When I was really really little, just a baby, someone took me to the doctor (I only had room for just the doctor's hand), and he stuck a needle in me after a count to three. Ouch! That was awful! But do you know what was in it? Do you have a thermometer, for telling if someone's sick? There's something in there, it's shiny and it looks like silver, *only it's not silver,* it's *mercury*. Mercury is beautiful, and *slippery*, and it floated up my arms, up up up, like clouds of floating metal, and all the blood was thinking "Hey! What's that? What's that going by, it looks like treasure!" And it went into my head. When you're a baby there's no stopping things from getting into your head, you haven't grown that part yet, the part that stops things from getting in. And mercury *loves* brain cells, it loves them so much that it hugs them tight and it stays there and not much that you can do will make it come out. I have mercury in me! Right now! *(beat)* Are you wondering how I know all of this…?

LUCY smiles.

My mother told me!

SCENE TWO

An abrupt lighting shift. MORRIS's *office. A few weeks after Act One, Scene Seven.* LUCY *is working on a drawing.* VIVIAN *has just come through the door. She is carrying some books and papers.*

MORRIS Vivian!

VIVIAN Hey, Lucy!

MORRIS You're here!

LUCY You're here!

MORRIS Great!

LUCY stands, puts on her coat. VIVIAN *is pulling out some papers.*

VIVIAN *(to MORRIS)* I have some things I need to go over with you.

MORRIS It's... it's five thirty.

VIVIAN Is it? I've been doing some research.

MORRIS You were supposed to pick Lucy up a half-hour ago.

VIVIAN *(to LUCY)* Lucy, do you want to draw for a bit?

> *LUCY sits down and keeps drawing.*

(back to MORRIS) She seems fine.

MORRIS Yes, but, Vivian, it's five thirty.

VIVIAN You keep saying that.

MORRIS Yeah, it's important that we stick to the schedule, we have to set an example.

VIVIAN Sure, yes, now I have some questions about Lucy.

MORRIS Uh, listen, it's the end of the day, and—

VIVIAN You have time to answer a few quick questions.

MORRIS No, I'm sorry, I really, I have to go home.

VIVIAN But you said we could rely on you, you said if I needed extra help, I only had to ask.

MORRIS The thing is, Vivian, you've been late the last two weeks.

VIVIAN Okay, yes, I've been working, I've been looking at autism triggers—

MORRIS Right, well—

VIVIAN —but it's very frustrating, there's a lot of conflicting information.

MORRIS Well, it's an evolving study.

VIVIAN But most scientists agree that there has to be a genetic *component*, at least, correct?

MORRIS That's the most current information, yes.

VIVIAN And they've been able to isolate a couple of potential autism genes, but—

MORRIS But there may be as many as a *hundred* involved, we don't know. Listen, Vivian, I really should—

VIVIAN   Now, there are no recorded cases of autism before the nineteen forties, is that correct?

MORRIS   It was named in the forties, but it may have been around much longer than that.

VIVIAN   Meaning that the autism gene may have been around for centuries, for millennia.

MORRIS   Meaning that in order for the rates to spike so suddenly—

VIVIAN   There have to have been cofactors.

MORRIS   Yes.

VIVIAN   Like mercury in childhood vaccines.

MORRIS gives a little laugh.

What's funny.

MORRIS starts to put his coat on.

MORRIS   It's just—. That's a very popular theory, but— Look, there's a lot of hysteria out there about mercury, and not a lot of proof.

VIVIAN   The symptoms for mercury poisoning and autism are shockingly similar, wouldn't you say?

MORRIS   Not all of them.

VIVIAN   Up until a few years ago, they were *still* using *thimerosal*, which contains ethylmercury—

MORRIS   Yes—

VIVIAN   —which is a *heavy metal*, / to sterilize the MMR vaccine.

MORRIS   *Yes, but…* Most countries have instituted protocols restricting the use of thimerosal.

VIVIAN   But not before forty million children might have been exposed.

MORRIS   Look, Vivian, the levels of autism have been rising at the same rate in countries that don't use thimerosal / as a preservative.

VIVIAN   There's also mercury in certain kinds of fluorescent lamps, batteries, ovens, refrigerators—

MORRIS   Okay, this is a complex issue, / why don't we—

VIVIAN   They use mercury to burn coal, did you know that? And it leeches into waterways, to be absorbed by fish, to be absorbed by—

MORRIS   Why don't we make an appointment to talk about these things.

VIVIAN   No, no, I just need a few more—

MORRIS   *I really do have to go.*

VIVIAN   What do you mean, where? Where do you have to go?

MORRIS   I have a wife, Vivian. She makes dinners for me. Usually very intricate, well-thought-out dinners. I have a very young child, who stands at the door waiting for me to arrive. I have to go home.

VIVIAN   Are you avoiding this discussion?

MORRIS   *Am I*—? No, Vivian, there are lots of people trying to figure out where it came from. I'm just trying to figure out how to fix it now that it's here.

VIVIAN   You want to fix it, but you don't even know *what it is* yet.

MORRIS   That's not true, it's just, it's *complicated*—

VIVIAN   You want to fix it, but you don't even know *where it comes from.*

MORRIS   —there are a lot of theories out there and not enough proof.

VIVIAN   *(sifting through her pages)* What about lead poisoning.

MORRIS   Maybe, but there's not enough proof yet.

VIVIAN   Gluten intolerance.

MORRIS   Not enough proof.

VIVIAN   Birth trauma.

MORRIS   Why don't we make an appointment.

VIVIAN   PCBs, pesticides—

MORRIS   What day is good for you.

VIVIAN   *Today* is good for me.

MORRIS   You know what, Vivian, I'm confused. / Lucy has been coming here for months—

VIVIAN   No, *I'm* confused—you keep telling me that you know what you're doing—

MORRIS   —and you choose to come in at the end of a session, / at the end of the day, and you're obviously upset—

VIVIAN   You keep telling me that you're on the *cutting edge*—

MORRIS   *What happened?*

VIVIAN   —but you can't answer any of my questions, clearly there are some *gaps* in your expertise—

MORRIS   Listen, we have a way of doing things here, / a very successful technique—

VIVIAN   *So what else are you missing?*

MORRIS   I'm not missing anything! / If you would just let me—

VIVIAN   You keep telling me what you *don't* know, why don't you tell me something you *do* know!

MORRIS   Why don't you tell me what happened, Vivian? / Otherwise—

VIVIAN   *Nothing happened!* / I just—

MORRIS   —*otherwise* how am I supposed to treat Lucy, how am I supposed to do what you pay me to do—

VIVIAN   Yes! / Yes, I pay you!

MORRIS   —if you keep blocking me, if you keep refusing to participate, because really—

VIVIAN   I just want you to tell me something you *know*.

MORRIS   Because really, it's Lucy that loses out, / in the end, if you don't—

VIVIAN   Just *tell me something you know!* Come on, you're the expert!

MORRIS   Yes! *Yes I am!*

> *LUCY starts to bang and yell. They look at her.*

(*quickly recovering himself*) No, Lucy, no yelling. No yelling.

> *LUCY yells, pounds the floor.*

No, Lucy. No yelling.

> *LUCY yells.*

> *He relents. She stops.*

> *A moment.*

VIVIAN starts to pack up the crayons.

(quiet) I shouldn't have raised my voice, that was unprofessional.

VIVIAN   Lucy, it's time to go.

Beat.

MORRIS   Vivian, look. Lots of people may be carrying the genes that are responsible for autism. It's not your fault.

VIVIAN doesn't answer.

Many things have to go wrong to make a person autistic. Even if Lucy was born with the autism gene, or the right combination of autistic genes, even if it turned out that she *did* have a, a genetic predisposition, it would have to have been activated or exacerbated by *several* environmental factors, *in co-operation*, and there was no way you could have stopped that from happening.

VIVIAN looks at him.

VIVIAN   What did you say?

MORRIS   I said it's not your fault.

VIVIAN   *(slowly)* You said many things have to go *wrong*…

MORRIS   …to make a person autistic, yes.

She stands.

VIVIAN   *A genetic predisposition.*

MORRIS   Yes, one that was exacerbated or activated by several…

VIVIAN   *(to herself)* Everything evolves, everything moves forward.

MORRIS   Vivian?

VIVIAN   Oh, *Lucy.*

VIVIAN kneels in front of LUCY, smiling at her.

Oh, Lucy!

Beat.

MORRIS   Vivian?

VIVIAN   Come on.

VIVIAN and LUCY hurry out.

MORRIS is left standing there, bewildered.

Lighting shift.

SCENE THREE

A week later. VIVIAN's home, in darkness. LUCY in a spotlight.

LUCY   *(out)* Do you see? It happens so quickly! She starts to talk. She talks
and talks, and says things under her breath, and she *laughs*. She is
working and working and pacing and pacing. And she writes very fast,
and she reads things out loud. There is so much to read now, so much
to look at! So many *books*! Books! Books! Books!

> *The lights come up on the house. It is messy, lived-in. Books everywhere.
> LUCY is on the ground looking at one of the books. VIVIAN has just come
> into the room.*

VIVIAN   Oh! That's my book!

LUCY   My book.

VIVIAN   Yes. I wrote that book.

LUCY   Bones!

VIVIAN   Fossils. Older than bones.

LUCY   Fossils.

VIVIAN   Good.

> *LUCY starts turning the pages.*

I'm, I'm going to sit beside you. I won't touch you.

> *LUCY does not respond. VIVIAN sits.*

These are all fossils of people who lived a long time ago. Millions of
years ago. You see?

> *LUCY is mesmerized.*

Look at the pictures. Interesting, isn't it. That's where we come from!
I mean, I'm assuming you're not a creationist, heh heh. I found that
fossil in Ethiopia. In Africa. That's a stone tool. They used that for
cutting. That's an animal skin, for holding water, or boiling water.
Those are caves that people lived in, and they painted all over the walls.
Isn't that amazing?

LUCY turns a page. Suddenly she points to a picture.

What. Oh yes, that's you!

LUCY   That's you!

VIVIAN   Yes, that's Lucy! That's who you were named after!

LUCY   That's who you were named after!

VIVIAN   Yes, good for you, Lucy.

LUCY   Lucy story.

VIVIAN   All right. She's very special. She's one of the oldest and most complete remains of a human being walking upright. You see? We know this because the distal femur is angled relative to the knee-joint surfaces, which means she could balance on one leg. Which is what you do when you're walking.

LUCY   Vivian, good story!

VIVIAN   Yes, it is a good story.

They turn a page.

She left us so many clues, just by dying where she did. And she died so very very long ago. That means that we're very lucky that we found her.

LUCY   Isn't that amazing?

VIVIAN   Well I didn't find her, but I studied her. She was only little, probably just over three feet tall. She was small like you, too.

LUCY   She was small like you, too. Lucy come over!

VIVIAN   No, she can't. She's not alive. She hasn't been alive for almost four million years.

LUCY   She's not alive.

VIVIAN   No, not anymore. But she probably had children, and they probably had children of their own, and on and on, for millions of years, up until the present. And maybe little pieces of her got carried forward, through her children, and through their children's children, and eventually— maybe—through me, into you. You see? This is where we come from.

LUCY   You see?

VIVIAN   I'm glad you like the pictures.

LUCY   My name is Lucy.

VIVIAN   Yes it is. Your father wanted to call you Megan.

LUCY   Not Megan.

VIVIAN   No, certainly not. Megan is a cheerleader's name.

LUCY   Hello, my name is Lucy.

VIVIAN   Yes. Good for you, Lucy.

LUCY   Good for you, Lucy.

> *VIVIAN laughs.*
>
> *LUCY laughs.*
>
> *Abruptly, LUCY puts her forehead against VIVIAN's forehead.*
>
> *VIVIAN keeps still.*
>
> *They do not look at each other.*
>
> *A moment.*
>
> *And then LUCY pulls away.*

I draw?

VIVIAN   Yes, of course you can. I have some work to do, too.

LUCY   I draw Lucy.

VIVIAN   Oh. That would be lovely.

> *The lights narrow on LUCY.*

LUCY   *(out)* Lucy! Lucy! The pictures in the Lucy book are wonderful. She let me take the book and read it and draw the pictures. I told her I wanted to draw more and more of them and bigger and bigger! So…

> *She produces a box of paints.*

Look what I got!

> *With a smile LUCY starts to paint the house.*
>
> *Lighting shift.*

SCENE FOUR

JULIA and VIVIAN in mid-conversation. It is a few days later. VIVIAN is hunting for a book. LUCY is still painting. She uses any colour that she wants. She will paint all through this scene.

JULIA   The European house sparrow?

VIVIAN   Yes. Where did I put it?

JULIA   What about the European—

VIVIAN   All the North American varieties of the European house sparrow come from a single breeding group that was brought to Brooklyn in the middle of the nineteenth century.

JULIA   *(She notices LUCY.)* Lucy…?

LUCY barks at her.

VIVIAN   Ah! Here it is.

JULIA   *(about LUCY)* Vivian—

VIVIAN   *(handing her the book)* And yet, in the space of only *one hundred and fifty years*, that group has evolved into so many different varieties, with so many variations in appearance, that it's difficult sometimes even for *experts* to identify certain subjects—

JULIA   —as sparrows.

VIVIAN   Yes.

JULIA   You're talking about—

VIVIAN   —evolutionary leaps.

JULIA   Saltations.

VIVIAN   Exactly!

JULIA   The Manchester peppered moth.

VIVIAN   Yes! Species that make rapid evolutionary leaps in response to multiple factors.

JULIA   Lucy, should you be doing that? Vivian, she's—

VIVIAN   Oh! Good work, Lucy, keep at it. *(back to JULIA)* Did you manage to locate that research?

JULIA hands over a sheaf of photocopies.

JULIA   Oh, yes, here.

VIVIAN is rifling through the articles.

Are you doing something for Lucy's school?

VIVIAN   No, these are for the book.

JULIA   These articles are about—

VIVIAN   I know.

JULIA   What exactly are you working on, Vivian?

VIVIAN stops rifling, looks at her.

VIVIAN   Think about famous evolutionary leaps, all right? Think about the seam between *Homo habilis* and *Homo erectus*, such a *huge* enlargement of the brain in such a relatively *short* period of time, right?

JULIA   Sure.

VIVIAN   What if a saltation is occurring *right now*. What if evolution is in the middle of making a *giant leap forward.*

JULIA   A *leap*?

VIVIAN   Yes.

JULIA smiles.

JULIA   Go.

VIVIAN   Okay. Basic Darwin. Evolution is the process of a species adapting to its environment in order to survive, yes?

JULIA nods.

But did he ever imagine that we would corrupt our environment so much that *we ourselves* would start to influence the basic matrices of evolution? What if we've been helping to make this leap *inevitable*, by obsessively meeting and exchanging and fucking—

JULIA   *(good naturedly)* Vivian!

VIVIAN   Thousands of years of this incredible collision of peoples, of races—this mammoth population explosion we've created on our march toward *civilization*. Do you get where I'm heading with this?

JULIA   I'm trying, sorry, I'm just—

VIVIAN   I'm talking about the fate of the human species.

JULIA   *The fate of the—*

VIVIAN   You said yourself it was only a matter of time before we found something.

JULIA   Okay, okay, *go on.*

VIVIAN   Now, civilization is a fairly new thing, it's only about—

JULIA   —ten thousand years old.

VIVIAN   Right! So that means that ninety-nine percent of humanity's evolutionary history has taken place in pre-civilized hunter-gatherer societies. We lived singly, or in small groups. But at a certain point, the discovery of agriculture makes food production easier, more efficient.

JULIA   Right.

VIVIAN   Suddenly a small group of farmers can provide for a whole village.

JULIA   Sure.

VIVIAN   The population *explodes.* Meanwhile, people who don't need to hunt for food develop specialized skills—the grocer, the policeman, the teacher, the politician—a web of interconnected people that depend on each other to survive.

JULIA   Civilization.

VIVIAN   Yes, but something's wrong. Our success has knocked the environment, the ecosystem, off balance.

JULIA   *(nodding)* Arguably.

VIVIAN   And with all our basic needs taken care of, we indulge in our emotions, emotions that we can't understand, that we can't communicate, and we can't control. So we fight, we make war, and we breed and we breed and we breed—

JULIA   I'm with you…

VIVIAN   And the more of us there are, the more we push ourselves to extinction.

JULIA   So *civilization—*

VIVIAN   —is a *mistake.* And we *know* it is, we can sense it—we know *we aren't meant to live this way.* But Mother Nature has a plan. To rebalance the ecosystem, before we kill the Earth, before we kill *ourselves off.* She *isolates us.* She diminishes our emotional vulnerability. She dismantles our obsessive need to connect, to interact, she makes us less interdependent, *she isolates us.*

JULIA   How.

> *VIVIAN grabs one of the articles that JULIA had brought over and hands it back to her.*

VIVIAN   There's been a *six hundred percent* increase in reported cases of autism in certain health districts in the last ten years.

JULIA   Vivian, wait a minute.

VIVIAN   We've contaminated the environment, that is the new reality. But maybe our genetics are evolving to adapt to the new reality, and succeeding.

JULIA   *Succeeding?*

VIVIAN   *It makes sense.* Genetic material mutates and evolves through generations, it's useless to resist it.

JULIA   Hang on—

VIVIAN   Or to question it.

JULIA   *Vivian.*

VIVIAN   *Think about it,* Julia. Survival of a species or of a genetic trait means by definition that it is successful. That's the nature of evolution: the *successful* mutations survive.

JULIA   *Jesus.*

> *VIVIAN gestures to LUCY.*

VIVIAN   Look at her.

> *They do.*

> *VIVIAN smiles.*

Six hundred percent.

JULIA   *(carefully)* Except… except that we're talking about a *disability*, here, Vivian.

VIVIAN   Life evolves, Julia. Sometimes beyond the scope of our imagining.

JULIA   Wait a minute, so, so people who aren't autistic are what, obsolete?

VIVIAN   If you want to put it that way.

JULIA   *Lucy can...* she can *barely* communicate, and you're telling me she's the evolution of the—

VIVIAN   Look around you! Person to person communication is becoming a thing of the past. We've become very clever at inventing ways not to have to speak to someone's face.

JULIA   You think because she can't express herself, she doesn't want to? People need to communicate, Vivian, they don't *want* to live in isolation—that's not *human*, that's—

VIVIAN   More efficient. Less room for misunderstanding, for conflict.

JULIA   You're serious about this. You really want me to roll up my sleeves and get to work / on a theory that's going to cause us to lose all of our funding, all of our standing, not to mention—

VIVIAN   Yes, yes I do, we both have to get to work. We need to assemble a team. We're going to need an evolutionary biologist, we're going to need—

JULIA   *Vivian,* no one is going to want to work with you on this! No one is going to want to associate with this theory!

VIVIAN   That's what they said to Darwin.

JULIA   You're not thinking clearly.

VIVIAN   *Come on,* have some *vision,* Julia!

JULIA   No, no, you've made a lot of assumptions, you—

VIVIAN   Look, maybe I haven't got all of the details worked out yet—

JULIA   *All of the details?*

VIVIAN   *Don't you get it?* Lucy isn't sick, she's *brilliant. She's the future.*

   Tiny beat.

JULIA   Yes. Okay. I have to say, Vivian, I'm, I'm uncomfortable with the general tone of this conversation, and, and as of late, I don't really, *I don't really recognize you.*

VIVIAN   I don't blame you. I didn't recognize myself until just recently.

JULIA   *(a dry laugh)* What, you didn't realize you were an evolutionary obsolescence like me?

VIVIAN   I'm not.

> *There is a short, terrible silence.*

JULIA   So you're autistic.

VIVIAN   Maybe I am. I think I am. Yes.

> *JULIA recoils.*

JULIA   Under normal circumstances I think I would laugh, but there is an *arrogance* to the way you've said that—

VIVIAN   Listen, Julia, I've spent years unearthing fossils, cleaning them, analyzing them, and saving them from decay and obscurement, but I couldn't do that for myself, I couldn't understand *my own self, my own bones.*

JULIA   But—

VIVIAN   *(over her)* Imagine you've spent your whole life in the dark about certain things, certain basic things about yourself, and suddenly you discover there might be an answer, a scientific answer to—

JULIA   *(sharp)* I *have* spent my life in the dark about certain things, Vivian. That's just life. Not everything can be explained with a theory, especially a theory that not only *excuses* what you are lacking in your behaviours, but *celebrates* that lack.

VIVIAN   That's, *that's incredibly dismissive.*

> *JULIA turns on her.*

JULIA   What do you want me to say?! I've devoted two years of my professional life—and my *friendship*—to you, and now you're telling me you're *evolutionarily superior to me?!* *Who's your inspiration—Mengele?*

> *Beat.*

VIVIAN   Jesus.

JULIA   I didn't mean that.

VIVIAN   You're fired.

JULIA   You can't do that.

VIVIAN   I just did.

JULIA   Vivian, no.

VIVIAN   You're fired. I told you I wasn't good at having friends.

Keira Naughton as Julia and Lisa Emery as Vivian
in the Ensemble Studio Theatre production.
photo by Carol Rosegg

JULIA   *Please don't.*

VIVIAN   I wouldn't want you to have to work with such an *ogre*, Julia.
Someone who *lacks* so many appropriate behaviour skills, someone
with such an incredible *lack* of perception. If you don't like my theories,
if you don't like my work, find another meal ticket.

JULIA   *Christ*, how can… after all this time, how can you be so *cold* to me?

VIVIAN   Interesting question. You can decide for yourself whether I'm
cold because I'm autistic or whether I'm cold because I'm just a bitch.

>   *VIVIAN turns away from her.*

>   *JULIA goes to the door, turns back.*

JULIA   Don't risk your reputation on this, Vivian. No one will stand
with you.

>   *VIVIAN ignores her.*

(*softly*) Goodbye, Lucy.

LUCY   (*without looking*) Goodbye, Lucy.

JULIA   *(to them both)* Goodbye.

JULIA leaves.

VIVIAN   Oh fuck. Oh whatever.

VIVIAN covers her mouth as she starts to cry. LUCY stops what she is doing and comes over to look at VIVIAN.

LUCY   You making a noise.

VIVIAN shakes her head.

You making a noise.

VIVIAN recovers herself.

VIVIAN   I'm fine. I'm fine.

LUCY gestures to her painting.

LUCY   Isn't that amazing?

VIVIAN turns around and really looks—for the first time—at what LUCY has been doing.

She stares.

The walls are covered with LUCY's painting. They look like prehistoric cave drawings. They are exuberant and colourful and impressive.

VIVIAN   Oh! Oh, *Lucy*. It's *beautiful*.

LUCY   *Beautiful*. Yes.

Lighting shift.

SCENE FIVE

LUCY in a spotlight.

LUCY   *(out)* Everything is changing! I don't have to do my faces anymore, and I only have to do baths when I have my blood. And we don't go out, and sometimes we eat with our hands, and we have lots of quiet time, very very quiet, and I can spin and spin, all I want. *Whenever* I want!

The lights come up. Split scene: VIVIAN at home, MORRIS in his office. MORRIS and VIVIAN are on the phone. LUCY paints.

MORRIS   You know Vivian, I think we present a fairly balanced approach—

VIVIAN   I'm not surprised you think that.

MORRIS   Can I finish my sentence?

VIVIAN   I'm not good at bullshit conversations. Isn't that one of the telltale signs anyway? Constantly interrupts? You were the one who put the idea into my head in the first place.

MORRIS   *What idea?* Listen, Vivian, it's been six weeks, I think you should come in and we should discuss this.

VIVIAN   Has it ever occurred to you that people like Lucy and I should just be left alone? That maybe we are better off alone?

MORRIS   Lucy and I.

VIVIAN   Maybe we don't need therapy, maybe we don't want to be brainwashed.

MORRIS   *Maybe we*— Vivian, are you trying to tell me that you think you're—

VIVIAN   It's a spectrum disorder, isn't it?

MORRIS   Yes but, but, Vivian, you don't have any *symptoms*—

VIVIAN   Difficulty forging and maintaining relationships, difficulty reading and interpreting emotional or gestural subtext, lack of emotional awareness and sensitivity, / obsessive and ritualistic patterns—

MORRIS   Okay, well, you certainly seem emotionally sensitive to me right / now, at the very least—

VIVIAN   And difficulty obeying the rules of polite conversation.

MORRIS   Vivian, listen, all of those things can be explained. I'm not saying those things aren't true, I'm just—. Look, it's really tempting these days to— OCD, ADD, we all have our categories, okay, and because of TV, because of the Internet, we can diagnose ourselves all we want! It's very dangerous to—

VIVIAN   You're missing the point.

MORRIS   All right then explain to me the point.

VIVIAN   The point is I don't care. And neither does Lucy. We don't care what your diagnosis is, or your anti-diagnosis. Lucy doesn't need to be in a place that is trying to cure her of her natural gifts.

MORRIS   *No one is trying to do that.*

VIVIAN   *I'm not just talking about her excellent drawing skills, Morris. If she doesn't want to talk, she won't have to. If she wants to* fixate *on something, she'll be able to. Because I will let her. Because unlike you, I don't think it's right to try and normalize what evolution has given her.*

MORRIS   *Evolution?* What are you—? How is she supposed to function in this world if you don't give her the skills to do that.

VIVIAN   Why should she function in this world, Morris? She is ahead of this world.

MORRIS   Has Lucy's father agreed to this?

VIVIAN   I'm hanging up now.

MORRIS   No no, please don't do that, we're not finished discussing this.

VIVIAN   You can cash whatever cheques you already have, but there won't be any more coming.

MORRIS   *(rapidly)* Listen, Vivian, what you're doing is, it may be well-intentioned, but it is not good *in the long-term* for Lucy, and—

VIVIAN   I'm glad you are trying to think long-term, Morris, that's exactly what I'm trying to do. Very very long-term. Goodbye.

> *VIVIAN hangs up. She rips the battery out of the phone and exits.*
>
> *Lighting shift.*

SCENE SIX

> *VIVIAN's home. LUCY in a spotlight.*

LUCY   *(out)* All right! This is the history of human beings! First there were apes. Then there were australopithecines (they had big ugly faces and flat teeth because they ate grass and bugs), but then they grew up, and then there was *Homo habilis*, and then *Homo erectus*, and then *Homo sapiens*. And one day, *Homo sapiens* will become *something else.*

> *She steps forward, excited.*

I am from the future! I am from the future, and I am so, so special! *(She spins.)* So special! So special!

> *The doorbell rings. LUCY stops spinning, looks at the door.*

Did you hear that? It's time. This is the end of the story.

> *Lights up on the house. There is even more clutter than in the previous scene, even more drawings on the walls. The whole house now has the appearance of a cave. The doorbell rings again. LUCY runs over, opens the door. JULIA is standing in the doorway.*

> *LUCY hesitates upon seeing JULIA. She reaches past her and rings the doorbell twice.*

JULIA Hello, Lucy.

> *LUCY ignores her and goes back to her drawing. JULIA comes through the doorway and goes to touch her.*

Hello, Lucy.

> *LUCY turns and gives her a short and furious scream, then resumes drawing. VIVIAN enters.*

VIVIAN What happened?

JULIA I just went to give her a hug. She's never acted that way with me before.

VIVIAN She's working, this is her private time. What are you doing here.

JULIA Vivian, I think—. I think maybe I have allowed my own issues, my own… whatever, to distract me from being a good friend to you, from really listening to what you've been saying to me. Especially that, that night. I really wish that I had… that I had put my own feelings aside and talked to you about Lucy, about your ideas.

> *VIVIAN stares.*

It's not about the job. Really.

VIVIAN I gave you a chance to be in on this.

JULIA Vivian, I just want you to talk to me.

VIVIAN Now I work alone.

> *VIVIAN goes to the door.*

JULIA *(quickly)* I got a call from one of the guys at the lab, he said they were packing up, they were closing down. He said he thinks that you're going out of the country, that you'll be setting up a new team there.

> *VIVIAN is silent.*

I asked him where he thought you were going, and he said he didn't know, but—

VIVIAN   This is none of your business.

JULIA   But *I* know. It's Africa, isn't it. You're going to Africa. With Lucy.

LUCY stops what she is doing, stands and stares at them.

LUCY   Africa.

VIVIAN   *Julia.*

JULIA   She didn't know?

VIVIAN   Lucy?

JULIA   When were you going to tell her, in the cab to the airport?

VIVIAN   Lucy? Are you all right?

LUCY   You're going to Africa.

JULIA   *Vivian.*

VIVIAN   *We are*, Lucy. *We're* going to Africa. To live. Together. All right?

LUCY avoids, moans.

Lucy?

LUCY   Lucy?

VIVIAN   Did Julia upset you?

LUCY   Africa.

VIVIAN   Come here.

LUCY goes to her.

Look at this. Look at what you made. *(She gestures to the walls.)* Look how talented you are.

LUCY   Look how talented you are.

VIVIAN   Yes. You're a beautiful, special, talented little girl.

LUCY   Africa.

VIVIAN   Yes. And we will have a house there, just you and me. And you can paint it all you want. And no one will bother us. No one. You'll be safe.

LUCY looks at her a moment, gives a short bark, then runs back to her drawing. VIVIAN exhales.

JULIA   She doesn't get it, you see that, don't you? She doesn't understand.

VIVIAN   I don't have to justify anything to you.

JULIA   Have you thought about this, Vivian, have you really—

VIVIAN   You don't know what you're talking about. You don't have children.

Beat.

JULIA   Yes, I—. Yes. You're right. I don't have children.

Beat.

VIVIAN   You can leave now.

JULIA does not move.

Julia.

JULIA   I should tell you something.

There is a knock at the door. Insistent.

GAVIN   *(from off)* Vivian. It's me.

VIVIAN looks at JULIA.

JULIA   Forgive me.

VIVIAN   *Jesus Christ.*

GAVIN   *(over them, from off)* I'm not going anywhere until you talk to me, Vivian. Vivian? Lucy?

LUCY runs to the door and opens it. MORRIS and GAVIN are standing there.

Lucy?

LUCY is frozen.

Lucy?

LUCY does not respond. He goes to touch her. She avoids.

(to VIVIAN) What's wrong with her?

GAVIN goes for LUCY. She scampers away and hides.

VIVIAN   What are you doing here?

GAVIN   What's wrong with her? What have you been doing to her?

They have made their way in.

VIVIAN   I haven't— I didn't say you could come in!

MORRIS   Let's not get worked up about this, we just / want to talk to you—

JULIA   They just wanted to / talk to you.

GAVIN   Lucy?

VIVIAN   *(to JULIA)* What did you do, did you just call him, or did you actually spring for the plane ticket, / is that more your style?

JULIA   Vivian, he's her *father.*

MORRIS   *I* called him.

VIVIAN   *(pointing at MORRIS)* You. You shouldn't be here. Isn't this against some kind of code or something, forcing your way into / people's houses?

MORRIS   Look, I'm not here to—

GAVIN   Lucy?

JULIA   Please, Vivian, just—

VIVIAN   *I didn't say you could come in here!*

MORRIS   We're just hoping you'll hear us out.

GAVIN   Lucy, are you okay? Let me look at you.

JULIA   Listen to me, we tried calling you.

GAVIN is trying to get a hold of LUCY.

VIVIAN   I had it disconnected.

JULIA   So what was I supposed to do?

VIVIAN   *Mind your own—*

GAVIN   *(over her)* Lucy, come here!

He grabs her. She screams and bites him. He releases her. She hides.

VIVIAN   Leave her alone!

MORRIS   Okay, let's, let's everybody calm down. Let's just everybody take a breath.

GAVIN is focused on VIVIAN.

GAVIN   I can't believe this, Vivian—*Africa?*

VIVIAN   Keep your voice down.

GAVIN   I *trusted you!* I sent her here so that she could go to *school.*

VIVIAN   She doesn't need school, she doesn't need therapy—

GAVIN   *What?*

MORRIS   Do you really think so, Vivian? She's back to screaming and biting—

VIVIAN   She doesn't scream and bite if you don't disturb her.

GAVIN   I sent her here so she could get *better,* not—

VIVIAN   She doesn't *need* to get better, she needs to be somewhere that she's safe—

GAVIN   —NOT so you could be free to take her anywhere you wanted, *least of all to Africa*—

> *LUCY gives a short scream.*

VIVIAN   Gavin!

GAVIN   *(over them)* —for God knows how long, *Jesus Christ!*

> *LUCY covers her ears and hides. MORRIS steps forward.*

MORRIS   Okay okay. Let's not upset her any more than she is already.

VIVIAN   Thank you.

> *A tiny moment. MORRIS steps forward.*

MORRIS   Vivian, please help me understand. You're saying Lucy doesn't need therapy, you're saying she doesn't need any kind of professional help.

VIVIAN   She doesn't.

GAVIN   *How can you*—

VIVIAN   *She has me.*

MORRIS   And you think that's enough?

VIVIAN   Your language is so condescending, do you realize that?

JULIA   No one here is trying to attack you, Vivian.

MORRIS   I'm just trying to understand.

VIVIAN   *(to MORRIS)* I don't care if you understand, *I know what Lucy needs,* we make sense to each other, *we're the same.*

GAVIN   *(incredulous)* You're the—

MORRIS   *All right*, Vivian, all right. Okay. Maybe I shouldn't discount it so quickly, this notion that you might be autistic. I don't mind admitting that I might be wrong about that, okay? Let's move forward with that idea.

VIVIAN   Oh, let's move forward?

MORRIS   Yes, let's get you some help.

VIVIAN   You don't get it, do you? I don't want your help. I don't *need* your help. And *neither does Lucy.*

MORRIS   I disagree.

VIVIAN   You want Lucy to be like everyone else? You want her to *fit in?* *She's perfect.* She's the future.

MORRIS   She has a disability, Vivian—

VIVIAN   And you want her to be *normal.* You want her to be a *normal* human being. Pathetic and desperate and confused and *destructive.* This planet has been *ruined* by *normal people.* Normal, *civilized* people have *scarred* this planet with war, and pettiness, and greed! Normal human beings aren't meant to be in charge, Morris. We aren't meant to live this way. It's *over.* Evolution is making us into something that terrifies you: people who can be alone, who *want* to be alone. People who aren't ruled by their emotions. People who don't subject each other to *every little feeling.* That's a horrifying thought to you, isn't it, Morris. To me, it's like heaven. *Heaven.*

> *Short, stunned beat.*

> *JULIA steps forward.*

JULIA   *(quietly)* Lucy is very special, Vivian, no one disputes that, but tell me: what survival advantage does she have?

> *VIVIAN looks at her.*

She. Herself. On her own.

VIVIAN   This is good, *you're* going to lecture *me* about scientific method? / You're an *assistant.*

JULIA   Because *she's not a trend*, Vivian, she's an *individual,* and in order for her to pass on her genes, she has to be able to procreate, and she has to be able to survive long enough to do that—

VIVIAN   You just don't have the *imagination,* / you never did—

JULIA   She has to be able to live in the world, Vivian. And as it is she can't cope without help.

VIVIAN   *Yes she can.*

JULIA   No, she *hides,* she *harms* herself—and that's not survival, Vivian, *that's not evolution.*

VIVIAN   Yes it is, you just, *you just don't want it to be true!*

GAVIN   *(exploding)* Bullshit! *Bullshit* it's evolution. *Bullshit* there's scientific evidence. There's no *scientific* rationale behind this, Vivian, and you and I both know it.

VIVIAN   I'm doing what you asked me to do! I'm taking care of her!

GAVIN   No, *you're trying to take her away from me!*

VIVIAN   She's not safe here, Gavin! No one understands her like I do! No one can see her for what she really is!

GAVIN   Listen to me, Vivian: *I don't care about evolution!* I don't care if she's the future! I don't care! *I love her.* I love her more than my own life, *and I have loved her ever since the beginning.* She's my baby. I'm taking her home.

    He moves toward LUCY, *but* VIVIAN *intercepts.*

VIVIAN   No! *No, she wants to be with me!*

GAVIN   I'm not leaving her here, Viv.

VIVIAN   Lucy, come here.

    VIVIAN goes to LUCY.

GAVIN   What are you doing?

VIVIAN   Ask her. Ask her, she'll tell you!

GAVIN   Vivian, *no.*

    LUCY has crawled out to her, terrified.

VIVIAN   Lucy, I'm going to touch you. I'll be firm.

GAVIN   *Leave her out of this.*

    VIVIAN takes LUCY's hands.

VIVIAN   Listen to me, Lucy.

LUCY   Silence please!

JULIA   Don't do this, Vivian.

VIVIAN   This is very important.

LUCY squirms.

LUCY   Gavin!

GAVIN gets down next to her.

GAVIN   I'm here, honey.

VIVIAN   Lucy, I know, I know I haven't known you for as long as Daddy has, but I know you now, and I'm so glad I do, okay? We didn't have our time before. It's our time now.

MORRIS   Vivian, it's not a good idea to—

GAVIN   Vivian, please.

VIVIAN   Is that what you want? Because if that's what you want, you have to *tell* them. *You have to tell them what you want.*

LUCY   Silence please!

GAVIN   You're *upsetting* her.

MORRIS   *Come on, Vivian.*

LUCY starts to moan.

VIVIAN   No, Lucy, you must calm down, you must tell them what you want.

LUCY struggles.

JULIA   Come on, *leave her alone!*

MORRIS   She can't do it.

VIVIAN   *Just let her speak!*

LUCY starts to moan loudly.

GAVIN   *What's wrong with you,* can't you see what you're doing to her?

VIVIAN   It's not me, it's you! Just leave us alone!

GAVIN   She's not safe here! She's coming with me!

VIVIAN   No, it's our time now!

LUCY starts to wail.

GAVIN She's not staying here!

VIVIAN Yes she is! She *belongs* with me!

GAVIN You're hurting her!

VIVIAN *She belongs with me!*

GAVIN *You don't know what you're doing!*

VIVIAN *She belongs with me!*

GAVIN *No she doesn't, Vivian!* YOU LEFT!

VIVIAN *(violently)* I MADE A MISTAKE!

> *A stunned moment.*
>
> *LUCY is cowering, suddenly quiet.*

I made a mistake, I—. I'm her mother.

> *She looks to* GAVIN.

I'm her mother.

> *LUCY starts to scream.*
>
> *All look to her.*
>
> *She starts to bang her head on the floor.*
>
> *GAVIN and VIVIAN lunge for her. VIVIAN gets there first and wraps LUCY in a tight hug.*

Shhh, Lucy, shhh. Okay. Okay. No more yelling, no more yelling.

> *LUCY struggles but VIVIAN holds tight.*
>
> *VIVIAN gathers LUCY closer.*

There. There. Very quiet. Very quiet. Very quiet.

> *Gradually LUCY settles.*
>
> *VIVIAN and LUCY clutch each other, very still.*
>
> *A long moment.*

(very quiet) Oh, Lucy. I'm sorry. *I'm sorry.*

> *A moment.*

GAVIN Vivian...?

Lisa Emery as Vivian, Lucy DeVito as Lucy and Scott Sowers as Gavin
in the Ensemble Studio Theatre production.
photo by Carol Rosegg

She looks at him.

(very gently) Why don't you let me take her for a while. Give things
a chance to settle down.

Beat.

VIVIAN nods.

I'm going to get her bags. I won't hurry. *(to LUCY)* I'm going to get your
bags now, Lucy. You're going to come with me.

GAVIN starts to exit.

(to MORRIS and JULIA) Why don't you give me a hand. It's okay.

JULIA, GAVIN and MORRIS exit together. VIVIAN is left alone with LUCY.

A moment.

VIVIAN   I'm sorry, Lucy. I thought… I thought I was—. *I'm sorry.* I love you.

There is a lighting shift. LUCY looks directly at the audience.

LUCY   *(out)* This is the part that I can't explain, but it happens. *It happens.*
We are alone in the room, all alone, and she says that to me, and her

voice comes out soft and broken. I've never heard it sound like that. She says to me:

VIVIAN I love you.

LUCY And, and, something happens that surprises me, something comes up from my stomach and into my mouth, and I am so surprised! I don't know what it is. It feels tight all over. *It hurts.* But when I hear her voice like that… somehow, I know what I should do.

VIVIAN I love you.

LUCY So I go down there, down down down, into my little cave, and it takes me a second to find what I'm looking for. Something I had tucked away down there, way down there in my little cave, where I keep all my things. And I hadn't looked at it in a long time. And there's not much of it, just a tiny bit, and it looks old old old, so old. And white, so white! There is only enough to give to just one person. It hurts. But I want to give it to her. It belongs to her.

LUCY takes out the white paint from her paint set. VIVIAN watches.

I never knew what this colour was for.

LUCY spills the white paint on her hands.

She walks over to VIVIAN, pulls her down until she is kneeling in front of her. And then, very gently, she puts her paint-covered hand to VIVIAN's face, covering her in white.

LUCY's hands linger gently on VIVIAN's face for a moment.

Then she steps back and smears some white on her own face.

VIVIAN Lucy?

LUCY looks at VIVIAN, then back at her painted hand.

VIVIAN stands. She is fixed on LUCY.

Lucy?

GAVIN returns.

GAVIN I'll call you in a few days, Vivian, once—

He stops when he sees VIVIAN's white face.

Vivian?

VIVIAN does not respond. She is staring at LUCY in wonder.

Vivian?

Still no response.

Vivian. Look at me.

She does.

A moment.

What happened?

SCENE SEVEN

The stage goes dark, except for spotlights on VIVIAN and LUCY.

LUCY   Vivian. *Story.*

Beat.

VIVIAN   All right. Yes.

VIVIAN turns to the audience and speaks.

(out) Hello. My name is Vivian. I want to show you something.

The lights slowly come up on the stage. It looks almost the same as it did in Act One, Scene One. This time, however, LUCY is in the picture with VIVIAN. She sits on the ground, a little ways apart from VIVIAN. She is playing with some of VIVIAN's tools.

Look at her eyes. Blue blue eyes like ice. My eyes are blue like ice.

The sound of a soft wind running through dry grass.

(to the audience) This is Lucy. This is my daughter.

LUCY gets up and comes over to VIVIAN. She hands her a rock. A fossil?

Oh! Thank you, Lucy.

LUCY scampers back over to her spot and resumes playing.

VIVIAN watches her.

Slow blackout.

End of the play.

A NOTE ABOUT SUBSTITUTIONS

The role of Vivian was written for an actress who had very blue eyes, and in the original production we were lucky to find a blue-eyed actress to play Lucy as well. If your Vivian or Lucy don't have blue eyes, the lines in Lucy's opening speech that reference their eyes—the ones that Vivian repeats at the end—can be amended in the following way:

LUCY   Look at her eyes! Dark and cool, like ice. My eyes are cool like ice.

Vivian would repeat this substitution when she comes to the same section at the end. We used this substitution in the New York production, where the actresses had different-coloured eyes (and neither of them had blue eyes), and it worked fine—it is simply more in line with some of Lucy's other more oblique, poetic references.

In addition, at the top of Act One, Scene Seven, if you do not wish to create Vivian's bedroom, you can have her sleeping in the main room. (She is referenced as a bit of an insomniac.) In this instance, instead of Lucy saying, "So I go into her room at night quiet quiet, like a quiet cat, and I look at her," she can say, "So I go in at night to look at her, quiet quiet, like a quiet cat."

This will also work just fine.

ACKNOWLEDGEMENTS

I owe a great debt to all the actors in Banff and Toronto who participated in workshops for *Lucy*—your input was invaluable. I am also indebted to Bonnie Green, Chris Scholey, and Katherine Grainger for their guidance and support in developing the play, and to Margaret Sirotich for her help in gathering materials for this published version.

It has been my great pleasure to consult with various autism and anthropology specialists during this process. Thanks to Suzanne Lanthier and Alycia Halladay at Autism Speaks, the staff at the Geneva Centre for the Study of Autism in Toronto, Maryke Hendrikse, Dr. James Hendrikse, and Josie Alaimo and Mariam Nargolwalla at the University of Toronto's Department of Anthropology.

For good ideas and very generous support, thank you to Don Hannah, Miles Potter, Sarah Dodd, Sarah Orenstein, Peter Paige, Eda Holmes, William Carden, and—as always—Shelley Simester.

Thank you to the staff and volunteers at the Canadian Stage Company in Toronto and the Ensemble Studio Theatre in New York City. Heartfelt thanks as well to Doron Weber and the Sloan Foundation for their support.

Great admiration and thanks to the original casts and designers in both Toronto and New York—your persistence and dedication enriched this play more than you can know.

Very special thanks to Karen McEwen, Larry Tobin and the students of the Lillian Street School. This play started with you.

Thank you to Iris Turcott for taking this play (and me) under her wing.

Thank you to my father for his enthusiastic support in general, and for *Lucy* in particular.

And, finally, deepest thanks to Andrew Kushnir for love and inspiration, and to the brilliant Seana McKenna, both for shepherding this play and for bringing Vivian to life with such precision, wit, and heart-stopping honesty.

photo by Ian Brown

Actor and playwright Damien Atkins was born in Australia and grew up in Edmonton. He has worked at major theatres across Canada and the US. He is the author and performer of two solo shows: *miss chatelaine* and *Real Live Girl* as well as the author of the full-length plays *Good Mother*, *Lucy*, and *The Mill, Part Four: Ash*. His plays have been produced at the Canadian Stage Company, Theatre Passe Muraille, Buddies in Bad Times Theatre (Toronto), the Grand Theatre (London), the Manitoba Theatre Centre (Winnipeg), the Stratford Shakespeare Festival, and the Ensemble Studio Theatre (New York). Damien has been playwright-in-residence at the University of British Columbia and the Canadian Stage Company, and he is a guest instructor at the National Theatre School. He is the recipient of a Dora Mavor Moore Award nomination for Best New Play for *Lucy*, an Elizabeth Sterling Haynes Award for *miss chatelaine*, and two Dora Awards for *Real Live Girl*. He makes his home in Toronto.